About the Author

Busby is a semi-retired architectural salvage dealer and unretiring writer of comic monologues, pantomimes and poetry. He is also the librettist and performing half of the geriatric tribute duo "Minge and Fackett" with their pianist, Vladimir Q Wildebeeste. Beside many ribald performances and recitals, the author has amassed a catalogue in his own write, of monologues and musings. Born in Birmingham's Balti Belt before the Balti was invented. Busby has lived the last forty years of his life in a leafy Warwickshire Parish, on a permanent building-site. His passions include village rugby, tennis, history, flea-markets, beer. An avid pork-pie collector.

"LIKE A MAD WOMAN SHITTING"

Look on the bright side — it could have been two copies!

Enjoy your raffle prize —

Busby.

Busby

"LIKE A MAD WOMAN SHITTING"

Monologues and Musings

Olympia Publishers
London

www.olympiapublishers.com
OLYMPIA PAPERBACK EDITION

Copyright © Paul Busby 2023

The right of Paul Busby to be identified as author of
this work has been asserted in accordance with sections 77 and 78 of
the Copyright, Designs and Patents Act 1988.

All Rights Reserved

No reproduction, copy or transmission of this publication
may be made without written permission.
No paragraph of this publication may be reproduced,
copied or transmitted save with the written permission of the publisher,
or in accordance with the provisions
of the Copyright Act 1956 (as amended).

Any person who commits any unauthorised act in relation to
this publication may be liable to criminal
prosecution and civil claims for damage.

A CIP catalogue record for this title is
available from the British Library.

ISBN: 978-1-80074-996-2

This is a work of fiction.
Names, characters, places and incidents originate from the writer's imagination. Any resemblance to actual persons, living or dead, is purely coincidental.

First Published in 2023

Olympia Publishers
Tallis House
2 Tallis Street
London
EC4Y 0AB

Printed in Great Britain

The Lawsuit

The church clock struck, and farmer Barty stopped to eat his snap –
A cheese 'n' onion sandwich that he kept under his cap.

The boiled egg in his pocket, with a slice of her game pie,
A dinner fit for champions; 'n' just watch the world go by...

At the end of a length of baling twine, his brown ale in the brook;
when a shot-gun crack then split the air, his blissfulness now shook.

The scattered crows, the fleeting hare, and his luncheon incomplete,
Before he'd figured just from where, a pheasant landed at his feet.

A lousy shot: the bird could trot, but lead shot had filled its arse.
Barty grabbed it; wrung its neck: and the bird had come to pass.

There appears a bloke in a track-suit. His Purdey still unbroken,
Points the barrels at Barty, and before a greeting spoken,

Yells, "OY! YOU SCRUFFY YOKEL! THAT BLOODY PHEASANT'S MINE!"
Barty simply drops the bird, and reels in his baling twine.

Knocks the cap off his Newky Brown, 'n' takes a long, slow swig.
"That pheasants landed on MY ground. I couldn't give a fig."

The Track-suit chap still aims the gun, but announces: "I'm a Lawyer.
I shot that pheasant from MY ground. You stole it, and I saw yer."

Well. Barty takes a swig of ale. "Fuck off, thee poncey git.
Yon pheasant here belongs to me. 'n' that's the end of it."

"I'll have you know," the Track-suit says, "I'm a lawyer for The Crown!
Renowned for winning lawsuits all over London town!"

"Is possession still nine-tenths of law?" says Barty, with a grin,
And takes a bite of his hard-boiled egg. "'round 'ere, a bad shot's a sin."

"I'll drag you through the bloody courts! You'll end your life in debt!
My fee's two thousand pounds an hour!" But Barty ne'er broke sweat.

"I tell thee, lad – this pheasant's MINE! So excuse me: in a hurry –
I've to hang this pheasant in the barn. I fancy pheasant curry…"

The lawyer flies into a rage, and fires off a warning shot!
So Barty simply turns around, and says, "I tell you what.
We can settle this right here and now. I'm a Burgess of this Manor;
Our old Court-Leet still practisin'… 'n' not even paid a tanner.
There's an old and ancient Bye-law called 'the kickin' of the nuts',
That's used for a settlin' o' disputes – that's if thee's got the guts.
A test of strength and stamina more effective than High Court,
I'm eighty six. I'm seven stone ten. You're a big lad; want some sport?"

"I'll have you know," the Lawyer said, "I'm a Cambridge Rowing Blue, and a Number Eight at my Old Boy's Club, and a tennis champion too!

I've never heard such prattle, but I'll have you, you old git! Just tell me what we've got to do, and let's get on with it!"

Old Barty marks the kicking-ground with a sharp stab of his heel,
Instructs the Lawyer, "Pick your end. Whichever side you feel:

9

We spreads our legs quite far apart. And each take turns to kick.
I ain't done this for forty years! An' I'm already feelin' sick.

We kick each other's knackers until one gives up as worst.
And according to the Bye-laws, the defendant must go first,

So brace yourself, you city wanker, you stuck-up So-and-So,
I might be eighty-years and six, but I'm prepared to have a go."

The lawyer's legs akimbo, with his hands upon his knees:
Barty polishes his steel-toe-cap on the leg of his dungarees:

He walks back twenty paces, and stops to catch his breath;
runs in like a West Indian bowler: (the one called "Whisp'rin Death").

And WHACK! He kicks his 'taters square. Lifts him off his feet.
The lawyer can but gasp for air: his 'breads now not so sweet.

Writhing, screaming for his mum, for Jesus and Mary too –
Collapsed, all in a sweaty heap, with the air completely blue.

Barty, meanwhile, takes his turn, with legs spread, for his shot.
And the lawyer staggers to his feet, with the meagre strength he'd got,

Saying, "Right you little bastard. Just brace yourself, you peasant!"

When Barty says, "I now concede. It's only a fucking pheasant!"

Moral: Weigh up your opponent, when you take them on at sport, and it doesn't mean you've won the case, when they settle out of Court!

The Fishin' Trip

It ain't so much a fishin' club; the only membership
is them 'as gives five quid a week for the Annual Fishin' Trip.

Three days two nights from the missus, all in one good company, with a mini-bus and driver, and a licensed B & B, and the hire of a boat and Skipper 'n the rods 'n all the bait, it was never for the fishin' that we all could hardly wait.

"We." That's me, and Ernie, along with Montague and Dai –
Chairman. Hon. Sec. Treasurer. Captain. (eh? a big wink of the eye…)
We have to do this trip for the survival of The Club
(we dreamt this up five years ago, in a lock-in at the pub)

… it's now an Annual tour of duty, for us diehard deep-sea anglers… and piss-artists, duckers-and-divers, and dirty-weekend wanglers.
There's lots to do in Morecambe, if your mind should stray off fishin'… there's lap-dance clubs and lock-in pubs, if fishin's not your mission.
There's snooker-clubs and bookies, and the girls are open doors
It's spring bank holiday weekend, lad! No cash, no hat, no drawers!

It's grab-a-grannie disco at the ballroom on the pier,
and happy hour all weekend. Everywhere, cheap beer.

Weatherspoons for breakfast, and at the B & B by lunch;
The landlady eyed us, staggering in; a rowdy-looking bunch,

Her booking said four pensioners from The Angling Society
(and her Boarding-House renowned for its decorum and sobriety)

Montague had pissed himself: or at least, he'd missed the bottle
and when Ernie pinched her arse, she couldn't pick which one to throttle.

Dai, with his brand-new dentures in, had a grin like Liberace,
asked, "'ave you primed the beer-pumps, lass? I'm feeling rather parchy."
Bags thrown on beds, and off we fled; Who'd want this barmaid's eye? ... with a hundred pubs in Morecambe, and two days to drink 'em dry?
We ended up, in the early hours, with a full day's booze on board – throwing pebbles at her window, hoping one of us had scored.

Come Saturday, we mustered, with our fishing crew intact.
None of us had scored, it seemed: we were ordered to get packed.

No full English breakfast; we got the laundry bill, instead –

And the discount lost for O.A.P's, just 'cos Ernie'd shit the bed.

We didn't need no knocking-shop! Dai informed her, plain and clear, as she swiped his SAGA credit-card. We left, in search of beer.

Weatherspoons! God bless 'em for their breakfasts and their ale.
For deep-sea-anglers such as we, behold the Holy Grail.

No need for accommodation, we can drink right through to dawn, and be up early for the fishing trip: first tide the 'morrow morn...
No less able-bodied seamen ever boarded any ship:
Full of beer, cockles, curry, with a desperate need for kip.

"We've an hour out, and all looks fine, we'll be fishing in the calm,
It's choppy now, we've a twelve-foot swell won't do us any harm."

Or so the captain told his crew, though it fell on deafened ears –
Trying to get life-jackets on, while draining the last beers...

Twelve-foot swell. Oh, fucking hell, you're up. You're down. You're up.
The captain 'd hardly cast us off, and Dai was throwing up.

Two day's beer and curry in the fathoms' depths beneath:

with a gummy, gaping open gob, Dai declared, "I've lost my teeth!"

And with his brand-new dentures now consigned unto the deep, Dai slumped upon the mizzen-deck, and soon was fast asleep.
Monty, me and Ernie baited up, and soon were fishin'
And all the time poor toothless Dai in comatose condition.

What a day! We reeled in cod, and when we stopped for snap Ernie had a brain-wave. (He's a right mischievous chap.)

He takes his teeth out, grabs a cod, and stuffs them in its mouth,
Says, "This'll give Dai a merry shock, when he thinks they've all gone south!"
So kicks Dai into consciousness, shows the cod; "Here, Dai, look, see!"
And straight away, Dai grabs the teeth, crying "Thank you God. Fuck me!"

Before our Ernie had the chance, Dai had stuffed them in his trap;
Then yells, "Oh, fuck. What rotten luck!" and there's our Ern's mis-hap.

Dai hurls the teeth unto the deep, cursing ,"They don't belong to me!"
While Ernie could but stand and watch his choppers lost at sea.

What a scrape. His merry jape, had turned out for the worst,
With Monty and me, hysterically, completely fit to burst.

But a well-swung cod across my chops sent my own set for a duck.
Montague's teeth were all his own, so he couldn't give a fuck,

And the four of us all in a fuss with the prank now not so rummy.
The captain turned the boat for home, while we argued, fought, all gummy.

Our fishing club disbanded: no more fishing-trip adventures
Never mind the fish we landed:
R.I.P., three sets of dentures.

A Romance in the Wind

At twenty-two, Miss Bickerstaffe was shapely, tall and pretty.
She worked in the reception of a law firm in the city.
Pin-striped geriatric types – silver-haired, or bald,
Her deep blue eyes and radiant smile enchanted all who called,
Behind her specs, not so much sexy, but simply efficient and witty.

Miss Bickerstaffe admired afar a public-school high flier –
the senior partner's handsome son, who winked as he passed by her.
His smiles she only took to be consideration, courtesy.
She never once considered he considered her *sub judice*…
'til he caught her ear, and called her dear…
"Dear Bickers… might I enquire…?"

He blushed, he stuttered, finally uttered, "Miss Bickerstaffe, I beg,
The Law Society Summer Ball, er, could we… shake a leg,
Er… accompany, I.E, you and me, could we go as a pair?"
Miss Bickerstaffe let out a laugh. "I'll have to do me hair…"
"Then you agree? Oh, Bickers! Jolly Dee, well, bugger me. Good Egg!"

She shopped determined to impress and settled on a low-cut dress
in black, of course, a slinky fit, the hem up to her arse, no less
with cleavage – just a little bit – stiletto heels and sexy hose,
no panty-line, a thong like twine, a blossomed summer rose.
She'd knock 'em dead, her mother said. And so she would, God-bless.

Come the day, Miss Bickerstaffe had fiffed and faffed and preened.
The hairdressers, the manicure, no food had intervened,
So early eve, her mum did grieve, "My girl, you've got to eat!"
And knocked her up baked beans on toast, let's face it, hard to beat...
"Ooh, Steve McQueens on Holy Ghost!" In seconds her plate was cleaned.

A Rolls-Royce honked its horn outside, her escort at the door;
Her escort gasped; Miss Bickerstaffe, as he'd never seen before –
A ravishing beauty took his arm, no fear of social gaffe,
Miss Bickerstaffe lit up the room, when she tossed her head to laugh.
Her sleek catwalk was all the talk as he led her 'cross the floor.

The menu had six courses, with Artichoke soup the starter.
The main course turkey, sprouts and stuffing, peas and

chipolata,
Brussels sprouts! No bum-hole pouts like one that's primed with Brussels
Miss Bickerstaff was clenching fast with all her sphincter-muscles,
A loop-the-loop of artichoke soup fermenting gastrically pro-rata.

Her first small indiscretion, she passed off as a cough:
Her escort sniffed, politely quipped that something might be off.
But rumblings off the Richter scale were grumbling in her vaults
Like Ginger Beer and Bi-Carb, washed down with Epsom salts.
A cocktail full-bottled, built up, being throttled, a bubbling Molotov.

Miss Bickerstaff excused herself and rushed off to the Loo wrestling with the thunderous fart that deep inside her grew,
Buttocks clenched to fight against Vesuvius a-coming,
The fart preparing to depart from deep within her plumbing.
The ladies' room couldn't come to soon... until she saw the queue!

Squirming in the powder-room with a powder keg inside her,
Like a bloated pig on syrup of fig with cabbage and rough scrumpy cider,
The only restraint for her angry complaint, a narrow silken gusset.
Fashion-designed, not double-lined, for a fart to blunder-

buss it.
She squeaked it, eked it, released it, on silent wing – like a glider.

The queue in the boudoir deserted; their nostrils all perverted.
Ladies with titles questioned the vitals of whoever'd anally squirted.
Poor Bickerstaffe was throttling back, her buttocks like a vice;
"Oh, my God! Call Dyno-Rod!" Was The Duchess's advice.
(To rod the sewer, or the evil-doer, she never quite asserted.)

If only could she, our heroine, flee, to fart in peace and quiet,
And rattle windows joyfully, with no offence meant by it!
At home, such feats of flatulence met rapturous applause,
Not bottled in the gusset of your Sunday-bezzie drawers,
Bickerstaffe daredn't cough or laugh.
She'd cause a bloody riot.

An open door, to a marbled floor, was worth a peep inside.
A library, in darkness… the perfect place to hide.
Not since the days of Mafeking was ever such relief…
The library's acoustics made a roar beyond belief.
A prolonged, and longed-for steady ripple. And then lots more beside…

A fabulous fart fortissimo that seemed a never-ender.
No fart did e-er its force impart from one so small and slender.

Its overture a mattress rumbling down an iron roof;
The concerto a vibrato of a thunder-clap, God's truth.
The final blast a trumpet-rasp; all her thong would render.

A light came on from a desk-lamp on a walnut davenport.
All hope was gone. For sat, thereon, her dashing young escort.
"Miss Bickerstaffe! You've caught me out! Er… It's just a crafty smoke.
Cracking fart. Right from the heart. I thought you were a bloke.
I tell you, you're the girl for me. Bickers, you're a SPORT!"

Jiggery Topiary

Madge Hopkins loved her garden, and her old man loved it too –
Until the poor sod popped his clogs in nineteen-eighty-two.

Since then, their little paradise was left for Madge to prune.
She did her best, but, laid to rest, her Ernie went too soon…

He'd turned their rough brick-ended plot into a true oasis
With nought but stick-it-in-and-watch as his gardenin' theory basis.

And yet it flourished – with love no doubt, anything will grow
But how she missed him – could see him now – the silly so-and-so.

Tending to his pride and joy – the sculptured privet hedge.
Or grafting like a coolie in the bit where he grew veg.

He'd talk his roses through the blights, the droughts, the wind, and rain.
To think that Madge would never see her darling Ern again!

She did her best, but, even blessed with fitness for her years,
The shrubberies grew rampant, the veg would end in tears,

The roses went to greenfly and her onions went to seed,
Madge Hopkins and the garden missed old Ernie's touch, indeed.

His pride and joy was a topiary fir groomed as an obelisk;
A Cleopatra's Needle, but Leylandii grows too brisk

And given many years since Ern took shears to his vision
It was not so much an obelisk, as a crooked imposition.

"I'll chop it down," thought Madge – but then – she looked, and came on sad.
The obelisk an obelisk no more, but – was she going mad?

The topiary fir, now nine-foot tall, was reaching for the sky,
And it took her back, an instant – to joyous times gone by.

That upright shaft – had she gone daft? Had took on Ernie's bend.
The one that made her bits go moist, could all her needs transcend.

She looked again – and at the top, the unpruned new-growth feast
Had fashioned Ernies helmet, or in Madge's eyes, at least.

She'd taken all her pills that day, and a sherry's hardly pissed,
but a crazy notion grabbed her that was too good to resist.

Ladders, shears, secateurs were soon all put to work.
Arthritis overcome by love, Madge Hopkins went berserk.

Who said Madge had Alzheimers? Her memory bank was fine –
Each contour, bulge, and sweeping bend contoured by love divine.

She chopped. She clipped. Madge snipped, equipped with all she needed – passion.
The body which her body worshipped all those years ago, she'd fashion.

The night-owl sang as Madge was putting tools back in the shed.
The clippings on the compost heap, Madge limped up to her bed.
Her body ached and creaked; she bathed, and let down all her hair,
then skipped across the landing, as if Ern was waiting there...

She slept the sort of sleep she knew, from times when Ern was tireless...
So deep she even missed the morning service on the wireless.

But what had really woken Madge was a commotion from outside –
Howls, hoots, and, "Oh my God!" She threw the curtain wide...

And there it was. Her handiwork – her topiary tour de force.
A nine-foot cock, erect, upstood – her Ernie's cock, of course.

Magnificent. A thick, green shaft, a bulbous head, with Jap's-eye. The vein she'd captured, root to head, the glands – all in Leylandii.

The screams from all her neighbours were a mix of praise and scorn –
With some you'd think they'd never seen the male organ on the horn.

Young mothers covered children's eyes, and others gazed in awe.
The dustmen voted Ernie's cock the best they ever saw…

Though artists, sculptors, passion-led, all hate the knowing critic,
Madge Hopkins got a rave review – not bad, for one arthritic.

There were comments borne of jealousy, some comments just politeness

But the dirty cow from number two,
Gertie, Val and Edna, just to name a few…
Madge wondered how the buggers knew
It was a perfect likeness.

Where Dragons Sleep…

1. The Meeting
2. The Mission
3. The Encounter
4. The De-Brief
5. Redemption

1. The Meeting:

The Chapel-house was bursting, and they'd all come from the pub...
And The Methodists, all three of them, with half the rugby-club,
The old stone church not near so full in nigh 300 years,
So the Vicar, back against the doors, rattled sermons in their ears.

Dai the Dead was first to speak: (our local undertaker) –
"The flood is coming! Save yourselves! Prepare to meet your maker!"
The baying crowd was called to hush by a knocking at the door
"It's that bastard from the Council," said the tart from Number Four.

A bowler-hatted Gent walked in, and fought the baying mob,
Midst cries of, "Hang him! Cut his balls off! Punch him in the gob!"
He raised his arms above him, and waved a set of plans –
"The Reservoir at Pant-y-Gog," it said. They tore it from his hands...

"That's our bloody farm, that is," Ianto Jones exclaimed,
"And the bloody place is damp enough!" his Mrs then

complained.
"Flood the valley?" piped up Huw. "And when? In months, or weeks?
What about the allotment, then? I've just put in my leeks."

"Above us, only water!" Reverend Morgan scanned the roof (not looking for the Almighty, but the Lead, was more the truth.)
"The rugby club won't mind too much; they can hardly raise a team,
And half the pitch collapsed last year into the old Coal - seam."
"And what about my Chip-shop?" said Dai the Fry, hands strung.
"Your fish'll be much fresher, Dai! You just need an aqualung!"

The map was passed from hand to hand, with cries all in despair,
"You can flood the bloody cemetery. My mother-in-law's in there."
The bowler-hatted gent piped up: "You fight this thing in vain –
All this valley was ever good for, is catchin' bloody rain.

They'll build a dam at Pant-y-Gog. And flood it when they like."
With that, he grabbed his plans and fled. On foot. They'd nicked his bike.
"We'll fight!" said Auntie Doris. We'll fight 'em in the Courts!"

They summoned up old Dai the Deed (a solicitor of sorts),
Who reminded them, "Don't panic, boys, you'll all get compensation?
And a council house in Prestatyn with half the Ukranian nation."
...but mind you, London lawyers charge a thousand pounds an hour,
while I get only half a sheep and a bag of Megan's flour."

"Then we'll fight with bloody pitchforks, they'll not take Pant-y-Gog,"
shouted Dai the Dip (the shepherd) well supported by his dog.
The chapel fell in silence as they all fell deep in thought...
"A prayer!" the Vicar proffered, with so many sinners caught,

but not one soul knelt down to pray, defeated though they were:
"It's not too bad in Prestatyn. They've got a McDonalds there."
They murmured and they mumbled, grumbled, knew not what to do.
When there came a shout. A child's voice, who was standing on a pew.

"We don' need lawyers! Don' need pitchforks, nor build a battle-wagon."
T'was Dai the Dim – the simple lad. "We've got to wake the dragon!"
Silence.

Ianto Jones climbed on the pew – "The boy is bloody right!
I know you dare not speak of it. Out of mind is out of sight.

Our fathers kept the secret, and our great-grandfathers too.
If we're going to lose our valley, then it's something we must do...
We must wake the bloody dragon. We must disturb his beauty-sleep."
"Ang on, you buggers!" said Dai the Dip. "He'll eat my bloody sheep!...

...and the poor sod that wakes 'im up. And anyone who's near..."
..."and anyone building reservoirs," said Ianto. "Never bloody fear...
A dragon sleeps a thousand years, give or take a few.
'n' the year the dragon nodded off was 1352,

So if you're proposin' pokin' 'im with any sort of stick.
You'd best be off that mountain-top, boy, pretty double-quick."

2. The Mission

A posse was formed of five brave men, and five men just plain mad.
There was three of Mrs Morgan's boys and their no-good drunken Dad,
volunteered by Mrs Morgan, not in pride, but in despair –
Once they got him up that mountain, they should leave the bugger there.

Dai the Hair (the Barber) had sharpened up his pole
And strapped it to a clothes-line prop, had blacked his face with coal.
Llewellyn from the Choir School was there to orchestrate
And brought two scruffy choirboys, to be used, he said "for bait."

With Dai the Dip as Captain, (because he knew the way)
And Merv the Swerve from the florists (to be the token Gay), With a cart filled up with crates of ale, Merv and Dai took stock –
And loaded up the final piece; the knocker-upper's clock.
"That'll wake the bugger up," he said, with a twist of the rusty key.
"I've set the alarm for two hours' time. You buggers, follow me."
With Mrs Morgan's husband, and the choirboys on the cart, they trundled up the mountain, each man up to play his part.

3. The Encounter

One hour and fifty later, they assembled at the lair,
Their path well -strewn with beer- bottles; Mr Morgan, God-knows-where,
the choir-boys singing Calon Lan – and swigging from a flagon.
"Come on boys! Less of the noise! It's no way to wake a dragon!"

The night-shift knocker-uppers clock was placed as near could get,
And a neat tick-tock echoed the cave as Dai the Dip broke sweat.
Dai the Hair prepared his pole: while Merv admired the length,
(and the Calon-singing Choirboys.) Said Llewellyn, "Give us strength!"

...and strength was what they needed, boys. The bloody clock went off.
"We're off to do the night-shift!" cried the Morgan boys, first cough.
A belt of flame burst from the cave, as the dragon cleared its throat.
The clock a blaring fire-alarm: got every bugger's goat,

ringing through the valley, while the dragon gave a roar
that shook them in the village pub, some seven miles or more.
The landlord called for time at once: "Come on you all, sup up!"
The windowpanes were rattling. "They've woke the bugger up!"

A dragon is a fearsome beast, if you've ever clapped eyes upon.
And Dai the Dip stared him in the eyes, all the others gone.
His sheepdog was the last to leave. For when he saw the beast,
Thought, "I'm buggered if I'll round that up. I'd want double-time at least."

The dragon came out three times the size, that would fit within the cave;
Its mighty tail despatched the clock, still ringing, to its grave.
A burst of flame scorched Dai Dip's ears, as the dragon gave a belch,
And to Dai the Dip's amazement, the dragon spoke in Welsh.

"Beth Y'wr Amser?" (What's the time?) said the dragon, half-awake,
"Pedwar O'r Gloch!" answered Dai the Dip, but the dragon said, "Duw's sake! *(the following a translation)*
I've hardly slept a bloody wink in four hundred years or more.

And was shitting through a needle with my arse and innards sore,

But put it down to simply being summat dodgy in my gut…
The Black Death it was raging, and I have to tell you, Butt,
I ate so many humans, I didn't care to check
The pink ones from the black ones or the bell around their neck.

…So I'm strictly vegetarian, and as for fighting saints,
Or holding captive Princesses. There're too many complaints.
I'm like most of us Welsh Dragons. We only want our kip.
That's why I ate the knocker-upper. Got right on my pip."

A big blue flame engulfed the beast, which set fire to the cart.
"Esgusodwch fi," said the dragon, "… but they also makes me fart."
The Pant-y-Gog village hero was all the more non- plussed.
"We kept your secret, Dragon. Now it's really shit or bust.

We've put up with your rumblin' an' told the folks it's thunder.
We've had the odd back-packer gone, and never thought to wonder.
We'll soon be under water while you're up here high and dry.
We hoped you'd save us from the flood…" A tear was in his eye.

The dragon's breath was fierce, and hot, but Dai just stood

his ground.
(his cleanest Sunday underpants, already felt well-browned).
"What do I tell the villagers? That you're poorly, sick in bed?"
The dragon slid back in the cave, mumbling, "Bugger Off. Drop dead."

4. The De-Brief

When Dai got back to Pant-y-Gog, the whole village were awaiting;
the survivors from the mission, with Mrs Morgan celebrating.
"Bara'r nefoedd," sang the Choir-school, to cheer his deliverance
(but it might have been "Delilah". He never could tell the difference.)

"Did you see the dragon, Dai?" The vicar crossed his heart.
"Oh, I saw him right enough," said Dai, "I even saw it fart."
"But will he fight for Pant-y-Gog? Did he say he'd do his stuff?"
"Nid ar eich Chwff, he said," sighed Dai. (which means not on your chuff!")

"The dragon's vegetarian!" Dai addressed the crowd, all shocked.
"He's sick of 'uman flesh he is, his plumbin's bloody blocked.
The worst B.O., I ever smelt. As a dragon, he's a farce.
The only fire that bugger spits is out its bloody arse!"

"I wondered where my cabbage went!" cried Huw, waving his hoe.

"The bugger ate my sugar-beet! my winter-sprouts!" piped Ianto.
"Where's my bloody barber's pole?" The landlord stopped 'em there.
"Where's my empties? Threepence each! Ten bob and we're all square!"

The lamps went out, and home to bed, the crowd slowly dispersed,
All hope gone; no Pant-y-Gog; Soon, all would be immersed.
Dai found his dog, still trembling, underneath the Shepherd's hut
"We'll take all the sheep to market. Then it's you and me, old Butt."

EXODUS

Two months passed, and not a day but leaflets through their doors.
(They lost count of the lodgers in the tart at number four's.)
The fliers prompting residents to claim for compensation.
And counselling available, to ease their consternation.

But Dai the Dip had no box to tick while filling in his claim
His place of work: just God's good earth, not signed to him in name.
The valley of his forefathers. Not even Dai the Deed
could give him proof of ownership or a title to succeed.

The bowler-hatted gent turned up, on each and every day.
The vicar first. A brand-new church? He signed up, straight

away.
The rugby pitch re-sited to a bog, where only hopes could sink
The Methodists (all three of them) had taken to the drink.

They all were moved to Prestatyn. With inside lavs, to boot, Re-named
"The Pant- y-Gog Estate" (or formerly "Beirut").
The landlord pulled his final pint. The church bell tolled the dead, (though it paid for a Ford Cortina, when sold with all the lead.)
Dai the Fry's new chip-shop van was bursting at the till, while the compo bought a caravan, four miles away in Rhyl.
And a supermarket! Which was handy, just along the street
– If you fancy Ukrainian sausage, Russian beer, or pickled meat.

And came the day, that Dai the Dip wandered Pant-y-Gog alone.
Empty clothes-lines, empty shops, not a butcher for Butt's bone.
The pub and school shut: every door now hangin' off the hinge
Just the Methodists in the playground swigging vodka, on a binge.

5. Redemption

A van pulled up, and stepping out, was the bowler-hatted gent
with a lanky youth, with a clip-board, who was on some mission sent.
The lanky youth, a graduate in Environmental Health
Wasn't looking for flora, fauna, but somewhere to relieve himself.

"We've re-settled every resident in the village of Pant-y-Gog, and I'm sorry. The state can't accommodate a Shepherd and his dog.
You've no papers. No certificates. No fixed abode. No proof that you've ever been employed, or schooled, or lived under a roof."

The bowler-hatted gent was smug. "...and soon, we'll build the dam.
That's every human being gone! Except you, Shepherd. Scram.
I'm off to pick some rhubarb. The Mrs likes the taste.
There's lots on the allotment, such a shame it goes to waste."

"Four hundred years we've been here!" Dai cried, knocking off his hat.
The bowler-hatted gent turned round. "We'll have enough

of that!"
"And you have been here far too long," Dai shouted at the man,
"but you'll not be going yet, look you!" The Methodists had nicked his van.

The lanky youth, relieved, enquired as to the ticking of his boxes.
The bowler-hatted gent informed. The "NO" box! i.e. badgers. there's NO foxes.
NO Natterjack toads. NO crested newts. NO bats of any sort...
NO bloody cowslips, NO marsh marigolds, flowers can be bought.

Just tick the bloody NO box! No tawny owls. No voles.
We'll poke their bloody nests out; we'll block up all their holes.
We'll spray the lot with weed-killer and then poison all the rest.
Just fill your bloody form in, lad; and let the council do the rest.

Dai rounded on the lanky youth, explained his local knowledge.
"There's life round here in Pant-y-Gog, you'll not find in a college.
The sky's been my university. I can read the Morning Dew... every cloud and buzzard-call."
The Pant-y-Gog Environmental Health Inspector (Supernumary entrance level B) stammered, "Phew!"

"Look here, you bloody shepherd!" said his bowler-hatted

Boss.
"You're standing in a reservoir. I just don't give a toss.
There's nothing worth protecting here, we're all as good as done."
"Then what about a Dragon?" said Dai, "'cos Pant-y-Gog's got one!"

The lanky youth, excited, quickly flicked through section "D."
"Dragon-flies... de dah dah, no. Dragon-wort... Ddraig?... Dragon!... Bugger me!
You say you've got a bloody... Dragon? All works must have to stop!"
Dai the Dip urged, "Come with me. Up to the mountain top."

The rest, they say is history. They abandoned Pant-Y-Gog.
The only person you might see is a Shepherd, and his dog.
But once in every lifetime, if you're ever there to peep,
You might just see a dragon help him, rounding up the sheep.

...and should you ever chance upon the sleeping dragon's lair,
there's a flaking barber's pole nearby. You'll know when you are there,
so do try to pass by quietly, and respect his habitat...
He needs his kip. Just throw a quid into the upturned bowler hat.

Pork Scratchings

What I'm about to tell you, my grandad told me true.
God knows what year he said it was — but it ended in a two.
A time when folk kept pigs at 'ome, fed every scrap and peeling,
Then had 'em butchered Christmas-time with no thought for their squealing.

But one pig that me Grandad had was more than belly-draft.
He slipped once in the pig-shit, and swore the porker laughed...
and when he told me Grandma that he thought the pig could talk she said, "Grandad, you saft beggar — it's just a lump o' pork."
But Grandad wouldn't 'ave it. He would tell the pig his tales,
like the time he'd backed a horse that won, or England lost to Wales.

and the pig a perfect audience. Snorting joy, or blarting.
Any mention of the Mother-in-Law, induced a bout of farting.
An amazing pig. So Grandad said, that when he got home from work,
as his key turned in the front-door lock, the pig just went berserk.

Would squeal just like a banshee, until Grandad would appear
with a cuppa, evening paper, and a fag behind his ear.
Sat upon a beer-crate Grandad talked about his day,
and read the news out to the pig, who'd hoot, or snort, or bray
as good as any donkey, or M.P's on their back-benches.
But "Jane Russell", "Brigitte Bardot"... he'd wolf-whistle at the wenches!
Gran's husband's animal husbandry, she claimed was over-zealous.
Grandad liked the company. Was Grandma getting jealous?

...which wasn't too unreasonable, thought Grandad, on reflection –
Gran had the same voluptuous bulk, the eyes, and the complexion...
One subject on their evening chats was Grandad's love for horses.
He'd ramble, mumbling on about the jockeys and the courses.

"Chepstow, going good to firm..." might raise a nodding grunt,
or the pig would give a snuffle to "... likes leading from the front."
The pig would snort, or grunt, or squeal at every bit of knowledge, hung on the form-book's every word, as though he were at College. Grandma couldn't disagree that the pig's interest was tireless,

"At least that pig's less bored than me. I'd rather have the wireless."
...and then it got to Christmas time. Tinselled butcher's shops.
Grandad's pig to soon become smoked bacon, crackling, chops...
gammon joints, four trotters, hocks, and the head boiled up for brawn.
No wonder then, that Grandad and his pig both looked forlorn.
"I'll miss you, pig," said Grandad, one cold December night, knowing that next Advent week, the pig would meet its plight. Then pondered on the Racing Post; a meeting due at Warwick. A grunt from pig, and then... a horse – "Alas Alack Poor Yorrick."
At Yorrick's name, the pig went wild and paced the old blue-bricks,

Squealing, screaming, like he'd copped the butcher's box of tricks.
"Alas Alack Poor Yorrick?" What had they chanced upon? Grandad squinted at the odds: sixty-six to one.

Worth a wager, sure enough, but all Grandad had put by, was the five pound-note to get the pig to slaughter-house from sty,

and the butcher's fee for chopping up his soul-mate into meat.
...and Gran would butcher Grandad too, if word got on the street.

The horse came in – won by a length. And when he told the pig,
It got up on its haunches. Danced, not your usual jig,

...but a tango, and a foxtrot. Grandad swore he really did!
And joined him in a Rumba... they were up three hundred quid!

Grandad told me this was worth at least a six month's wages.
He told no one, except the pig. Then scoured the racing pages.

"Kempton Park," read out the card, which hardly raised a snort.
but Newmarket, the going hard, the jockey Pat McCourt,

and once again the pig went wild, when he said the horse's name –
they stared at one another. The horse was called "Je t'aime."

A mutual grunt. A worthy punt, "Je t'aime", thirteen to two.
It came in by a country mile, and Grandad's fortune grew.

Grandad's army saddle-bag was bursting with the loot.
Enough to pay the mortgage off, and the tally-man, to boot.

But yet again, the pig went wild when Grandad read the form,
So he put the entire saddle-bag on the nose of "Thunderstorm."

"Thunderstorm" joint-favourite, at odds of five to two,
the going given good to firm, on a course the horse well-knew,

the jockey and the trainer all approved by oinks, and snorting and squeals so loud, the neighbours said such cruelty needs reporting.

...and sure enough, old "Thunderstorm" outstripped 'em from the gate.
Five thousand in the saddle-bag, Grandad could hardly wait

to get back home, kiss wife and pig, go out and celebrate.
If only Grandad hadn't missed a most important date...

Gas-lamps lit the cobbled street, with Grandad's home in sight,
Grandad much the worse for wear, but soon would be all right,
When the Mrs saw his saddle-bag, she'd excuse him for his flutter…
Outside the door, poor Grandad saw blood floating in the gutter.

And straw across the paving-slabs, with whiskers, hair, saliva.
…and Grandma's opening the door with, "You owe me a fiver,
it's knackers-day." Today, the day, the pigs all went to slaughter!
Grandad buckled at the knees, and his eyes began to water…
and Grandad's face so drawn and grey, as though he'd seen a ghost, was Grandma's confirmation, that he loved the pig the most.

But the contents of the saddle-bag… she thought he'd robbed a bank!
"No banks been robbed," poor Grandad sobbed, "You've got the pig to thank."

Grandma strictly Methodist – never gambled, cursed, got merry.
"But You beat the bookies? Bloody hell! Bugger – where's the sherry?"
Grandad wasn't listening… Grandad was on his crate.

Holding court – in tears, distraught, at losing his best mate.

The pig returned to Grandad's house, no longer wild and skipping;
Black pudding, bacon, labelled up, and jars and jars of dripping.
Kidneys, liver, sausage, joints. "A pig is quite incredible,"
as Grandad said, "from tail to head, the squeal's all that's inedible."

...and something else that Grandad said is "A secret is a curse."
A secret kept from pig, and wife – could only make things worse...
No, never mind the tug-of-love twixt livestock and the wife,
Or the secret in the saddle-bag that would set them up for life...

Grandad and Grandma never got to raise a Christmas toast,
With roast turkey on the menu – or a bungalow on the coast.
Grandad's trip to the savings-bank is where this sad plot thickens...
He lost the lot on a real hot-shot that he got from next door's chickens.

Arthur's Last Day

Arthur was a milkman whose career spanned sixty years
And now was on his last day, as he fought to hold his tears.
With every bottle dropped he stopped, to pick up cards, and gifts,
from appreciative Clientele – on this last of many shifts.

His milk-float cab was heaving with the presents he'd received
And the envelopes well-stuffed with notes he'd never have believed,
But one more street, the round complete, his milkman life was through.
Just a cash-in at the depot, and attend his leaving "do".

A dozen doorstep drops at most, and Arthur would be done, but one last call filled him with dread. The cow at Thirty-One.

Of all his many customers, this one had been a curse;
A moaning, sour-faced rotten bitch as attractive as a hearse.
She never called him Arthur, just "the milkman" or "oy, mate!" Her order either wrong or late, or he didn't shut the gate.

So as he grabbed two semi-skimmed, and checked the dozen eggs, Arthur trod the flagstone'd path on his weary, bandy legs...
The door was opened sharply, and caught him unawares.
"Hello there Arthur, darling! Get up them bloody stairs!"

In suspender-belt and stockings, with crutchless satin pants
she flung poor Arthur up the stairs. He didn't have a chance.
His uniform ripped off his bones, his long-johns round his knees,
She exercised her fifteen stones in knowing how to please,

And gave him her full repertoire, and drained the old boy dry.
He fell into a blissful sleep, with a twinkle in his eye.
...and dreaming still of his escapade, his sensual dreams were shaken
by the curdling yell of the bird-from-hell and a smell of burning bacon.

"Oy! Milkman! Get your arse down 'ere – your eggs are nearly ready!"
Arthur ventured to the kitchen, with his bandy legs unsteady.
On the table was full-English, with marmalade and toast
And lounging on the cooker, his suspender-belted host.

But also, Arthur noticed, was a pound coin, centrepiece.
A saucer with a pound coin on, in a splash of bacon-grease.
Bemused, balls drained, bewildered, he meekly took his chair,
And eyed her bursting lingerie, with her wild bed-tousled hair...

"Come on, you old git! Hurry up. Me 'usband's workin' nights
An' he's bound to spot the ladder in me brand new fish-net tights."
Arthur tucked in heartily, with an appetite well worked up
And eyed the pound coin sat there, as he downed his last tea-cup.

"Thanks for that," said Arthur, "and also for the treat.
But tell me you old rat-bag, why? You're the nightmare on this street."
"You old ungrateful bastard!"
she retorted, "you old clot... I knew you were retiring, so I asked my 'usband what... remuneration I should leave. So just you listen here...
He told me, Fuck him. Give him a quid.
The breakfast was my idea!"

Fuel for Thought

Now Finbarr bought this boiler t'ing off the guvernment website.
A feckin' massive yoke it was; t'would keep him warm, all right;
A "bio-mass converter" as dem greenies like to call it.
Costin' eighty t'ousand quid, and a fortune to install it.

But the money troubled Finbarr none: he bought it on the credit.
A t'ousand down and the same each month set up on direct debit.
The R H I, (dat's renewable heat, an' the "I" is for "incentive"),
provided for the likes of Finn's accounts to be inventive…

A feckin' giant of a boiler, that filled the milkin' shed,
which didn't bother Finbarr, what with dairy farmin' dead.
An' another feckin' great machine, to mash logs into splinters
was crammed into the winter store, and fuck the feckin' winters.

Drive past Finn's farm at Christmas, you could feel the feckin' heat
Four hundred yards or so away, they wore t-shirts in the

street.
'n' anyt'ing we wanted burned, we took to Finbarr's farm –
Hedge-cuttin's, wardrobes, t'ree-piece suites. Anyt'ing. No harm.

Black bin-bags of personal stuff. Tax demands, returns.
Anyt'ing you want shut off. Anyt'ing that burns.
The odd dead cat. Asbestos sheets. All reduced to ash.
And every month, the guvernment pays ol' Finbarr out in cash.

Four t'ousand quid, to be precise. Ol' Finbarr did his sums.
He's up some forty-t'ousand quid whenever Christmas comes.
'n' don't include the drinks and tips, for the gettin' rid of shite…
I tell you, workin' out Finn's take would keep you up all night.

A bio-mass converter! 'Tis efficient in extreme:
Burns shite destined for land-fill – every greenie's dream.
Be-Jeezus, sure, Ol' Finbarr surely wouldn't ever hug a tree
But he cut right t'ru the red tape most eco-logic'ly

The RHI inspector's ashes scattered wid respec's
The DEFRA yout' in his cashmere suit incinerated next
'n the Independent Auditor, wid his pencil in his gob,
was shrouded with some underfelt from a local roofin' job.

The calorific value of crematin' human trouble produced a
co-efficient that saw Finbarr's income double…

'n' a certificate awarded, which Finn hung up in the loo –
The poor sap who delivered it then contributed, too.
The vat inspectors, debt collectors, found Finn's fire door.
A Jehovah's witness once a week – they jus' keep sendin' more.

But there came an end to our fiendish friend an' his passion fer recyclin'
Finn's need for fuel was ne'er so cruel when he threw Reveren' Father Michael in.
For Reverend Father Michael had been out for his walk.
When passin' by Ol' Finbarr's farm, he got the smell o' pork.

An' this day bein' Friday when good Catholics dine on cod,
He marched across the farmyard, did our fiery man of God.
He saw Finn at the fire-door, chucking in a checkered hat. A traffic-warden's cap, it seemed, a familiar one at that;

No sooner did he genuflect, did Ol' Finbarr grab yer man an' pushed the Reverend Father in, to where it all began…
The rosary beads were rattlin' like marbles on the floor,
An' Finbarr skatin' in his boots an' thru the fire door. Which goes to show that good or bad, should we burn in hell,
the calorific values' just the same. We all burn just as well.

A Reunion Perchance

A busy corner Starbucks, and in a window-seat,
an Armani-suited lady sits and stares out to the street.
Manicured, brunette-coiffured, well-heeled (Jimmy Choos),
Sips her coffee, flicks her iPhone, thumbing through the news.

She drops her phone, distracted, by a girl outside the door –
A skinny figure, long-flowing hair… someone she's seen before?
The girl's wrapped in a cardigan, both elbows showing skin,
her Levi's worn and faded, and her sneakers wearing thin.

Armani girl then stalks her, as she comes into the shop,
hears her order coffee: the penny begins to drop…
So, as the Cardie'd girl turns round, they catch each other's eye –
and instant recognition! Oh my, oh my, oh my!

Schoolgirl friends, they hadn't met in over fifteen years,
Once totally inseparable, now both in joyous tears.
They hug, then take a table, with each one just as keen
to hear the other's story of the years gone in between.

Armani girl describes a life exceedingly well-blessed –
Houses in Chelsea, Cornwall, Nice; fast cars and all the rest.

Her bloke a city financier who she'd met while still at uni,
as rich as bloody Croesus and as handsome as George Clooney.

Her kids at some posh public school, but hey, girl! That's enough!
(not wishing she should rub it in, with her old mate looking rough)
The cardigan-girl rolled up her sleeves, and told a different life:
Phew! an ever-uphill struggle for her fifteen years a wife.

She was about to go to uni when he knocked her up with twins;
Her bloke a pigeon-fancier, who was working on the bins.
And wouldn't swap it for the world: Would do it all again.
"He loves the kids, and still loves me. We might be skint, but then...

I wouldn't call him handsome, but one thing you'd not expect:
He can perch four pigeons on his dick when it's standing up erect!"
Upon this news the Armani girl collapsed, in tears, distressed;
"Whatever's up, girl? What's up, Lass?"
Armani girl confessed:

"I've an interview at Tesco's. I've lied. This suit's a sham.
I'm in a bedsit, just nearby. Completely broke, I am.
The Alco I married's mega-rich; that, at least, was true."

He took off with his secretary, and beat me black and blue.

"Please forgive me!", poor Armani sobs, into her Hermes scarf.
Schoolmate in the cardie, says, "Come on, you really have to laugh –
I've lied, just as much, I have! Your forgiveness, too, I beg –
I lied about the pigeons… One of 'em 'as to stand on one leg!"

Maureen's Bike

Maureen ordered the bike with intention to ride it;
enthused at the quality, stood there, astride it.
The full-enclosed skirt-guard: a sprung-saddle in leather;
a bike for a lady, whatever the weather.

Caliper brakes, Sturmey-Archer three-gear
A basket up front, and a rack to the rear.
Dynamo lighting. An old sit-up-and-beg
frame bespoke; made to measure, her inside leg.

With her feet on the pedals, off Maureen went
down the hill to the shop, on a mission hell-bent,
announcing the start of her self-propelled freedom.
She'd fetch her own fags whenever she'd need 'em.

From the moment she ordered the coach-painted livery,
She told all of the freedom that came with delivery.
She'd cycle each morning for croissants and papers,
Stopping for chats with all of the neighbours,

She'd cycle with Grandkids to take 'em to school…
With the stop at the shop for some sweets as the rule…
and a whole world ahead of her, pedalling free.
Off she went, down the hill; her maiden sortie.

The sound of her tinkling bell gone from our ears…
Maureen off on her own after all of these years.
She'd be off on her travels whenever she'd like,
No go-fers or chauffeurs. She'd now got a bike…

The dust hadn't cleared when we saw, down the track,
the bike being pushed as she made her way back,
Maureen's cussing made clear, no skate in the park,
for all we could hear was, "Sod that for a lark!"

Ceremoniously dumped, without propping the stand,
With no care for the state or the place it might land,
She lit up a fag and strode off in a huff.
Maureen a cyclist? Not on your chuff.

Thirty years later, and Maureen long gone, though in some
disrepair, her Raleigh lives on.
Chained to the railings, the hub-key long lost, her frame lost
to ivy, the saddle now mossed,
The brambles and nettles concealing the green
stove-enamel of Maureen's self-powered machine;
the rubber tyres perished, though still deep in tread.
Nought point two miles, the mileometer said.

And nought-point-one miles, not ridden, but pushed
before banishing bike and intentions to rust.
Godbless dear old Maureen, and long live her bike.
They'll both live forever, and do as they like.

Sing along a Menopause

(Any Cream Will Do) With apologies to Sir Tim Miles Bindon Rice

Oh there are times
When copulation
Needs lubrication
Just to oil the flue,
And at my age
Full penetration
Needs lubrication
'n' any cream will do.
Used chip fat oil
Is nice and greasy
It slips in easy
With a splash or two.
When things get rough
Don't hide your shyness
When it comes to dryness
Any cream will do.
A gob of lard
A tub of marge
Some axle grease
Or crème fromage
Swarfega, Johnson's Wax 'n' Shine
Will help things slip 'n' slide!

But just last night,
It would not glide up
I'd completely dried up
And before I knew
I grabbed a tube
Straight off the table
Didn't read the label
Used a squirt or two
It didn't work;
I squirted more in
And more and more in
Any cream will do.

When all at once
mid-copulation,
a strange sensation
simply grew and grew…
A scream of pain
A cock aflame
I stood there
pissing acid rain
Bollocks blistered, farting fire
We found the empty tube.
"Wear safety gloves.
Use extreme caution.
just a tiny portion
for a cooker like new."
Don't fill your twat
With oven cleaner
Use something greener
Any cream will do;

A squirty tube
With salad cream in
When mixed with semen
Could launch the QE II;
The grinding paste
You clean the hob with
Don't smear his knob with
But any cream will do.

A gob of lard
A tub of marge
Some axle grease
Or crème fromage
Swarfega, Johnson's Wax 'n' Shine
Will help things slip 'n' slide!
Repeat verses 1 and 2 along with the cream.

The Scottish Midge

Culicoides Impunctatus – Miniscules Stoppitbitenus

Whin yir skin comes oot in lumps 'n' bumps
'n' gangs all red and swellin'
'n' yir fizzog burstin' oot like mumps
– tae the heavens ye are yellin'
'n' yir itchin' tae distraction
like a moggie wi' the fleas
then we'll give nae satisfaction
e'en wi' a pretty-please.
Wi' a fighting weight sae miniscule,
A fraction o' a feather
Wi' a bayonet o' stainless steel
Wid pierce the thickest leather.
Each clood ay'us a mullion-strong,
Wi'in a fly-swat's arc.
Each ayn ay'us a gnat's chuff long,
Wi'r boond tae hit oor mark.
C' mo'on! Ye whinin' Sassenachs,
We love yir rottin' meat.
Yir rottin' sweaty bum-cracks
'n' yir manky reekin' feet.
We divnae gi' a flyin' fuck
Fir yir midge-repellant creams

Sorry, pal, yi'r ootae luck.
We'll stick ye in yir dreams.
Nae fightin' force the whole world o'er
Cuid tak' oor braggin' rights
That leaves oor enemy's skin sae soor
An' keeps 'em up at nights.
Nae fightin' force yid ne'er despatch
Cuid flicht through any keyhole
'n' penetrate yir privy patch,
yir arsehole or yir earhole.
Ye widnae think a buzzin' mist
Cuid cause yir flesh sich strife,
Ask any entymologist –
Run fir yir fuckin' life!

P.S. Have You Made a Will?

Wrapped up in a blanket, she sips at her tea,
her feet at the gas-fire (turned down to mark 3).
In fingerless gloves she nibbles at toast.
The letter-box rattles! And clatters. Her post.
All sizes of envelopes, heaped on the floor, with a couple of
jiffy-bags stuffed in the door. The first has a soft toy, from
China – a panda. She smiles at the cuddly gorilla. (Rwanda).
The gorilla and panda are lovingly propped
with the foam-filled endangered she chose to adopt,
the mantlepiece crowded with toy blind-dog pups,
and bears of all sizes, snow-leopard cubs,
midst pictures in frames, of t-shirted kids,
smiling and waving. No fly-crusted eyelids,
which would cheer any benefactor no end.
Her family. They need her, their faraway friend.
The donkeys. The images prey on her mind,
hobbling and crippled. Thank God she signed
up for four quid a month, for in the next letter
there's news that poor Pedro is looking much better!
A photo-shopped note says her proxy step-daughter,
Ngomi, no longer drinks pox in her water,
But, "Dearest, sponsor. We DO appreciate…" … while
enclosing a fresh Direct Debit Mandate.
She answers Ngomi. One page, short and sweet. "Your
English is good. Your writing so neat! I'm so glad that the

water's no longer a trek.
Many thanks for the update." And writes out a cheque.
...Views the rest of her mail on the chintz table-cloth, turns on the telly, warms yesterday's broth,
and supping, considers the post yet outstanding – The statements. Reminders. Arrears. All demanding.
And what of her savings' reducing amounts?
She's living, surviving. It's giving that counts.
On the telly, there's elephants bleeding in chains.
The gas-bill outstanding the least of her pains.
She's adopted a family. Someone to share
her concern, her desire for a world that's out there, but as helpless as any poor orphaned bull-calf, the one that's most needy, is her, by a half.

Miracle Gro

I wandered lonely as a cloud, and gazed within my shed,
I know not where: I simply gazed, got lost within my head.
When all at once, devoid of thought, I reached and took a swig
of Buxton's finest water, sprung... at least, I thought I did.
A numbness pained my senses, as if hemlock I had drunk,
but a mixture far much worse than that; cat-piss flavoured gunk.
Not earth-sprung mineral water, but a tincture made in hell:
"Miracle Gro." For flowers and fruit. It don't half make 'em swell.
...but as a light refreshment, well, I cannot recommend it.
A taste so sour that a good lunch-hour of ale still failed to end it...
An accidental overdose of a mineral-boost for plants,
"For bloom, for growth, for strength," it said.
The Mrs checked my pants.
Her usual derision was replaced by haughty cackle,
as the Mrs gave inspection of my mineral-boosted tackle.
"It hasn't grown a bit." She laughed. "But it shines a lovely colour.
Radish... plum... no! beetroot-red. It used to be much duller."
My pubic hair, the Mrs said, had curled beyond belief –
Not like the moulted, withered strands that once stuck

between her teeth.
I grabbed my vest – surveyed my chest – and bugger me – a bush.
Ear-holes, nostrils, arsehole, too. An arboretum, at a push!
My old school rule revealed my tool unaffected by the mix.
The inadequate four inches (that the Mrs thought was six).
My balls, not shrunken walnuts, but now a pair of plums…
Or damsons. No miracle growth, according to my sums.
Wee sleekit, cow'rin timrus beastie, oh wit a panic's in thy nestie!
A nestie bursting o'er mah strides and oot mah pants'n vestie.
I shaved and clippered twice a day, and the bits I couldn't see, With a mirror and a blow-torch, the Mrs razed for me…
…but my baby's bum did soon become the arsehole of a Yeti –
I could comb and plait the armpits, and it made 'em twice as sweaty.
Nostrils, beard and eyebrows merged and burst, all cornucopiary,
exfoliatory attempts reduced to nought but fuckin' topiary.
Reluctantly conceded that drastic measures needed, I agreed to see the Doc.
His hilarity receded, amid giggling fits, he pleaded, "Has it done much for your cock?"
The flower-feed, we both agreed, was not a threat to life.
…and my cock no threat to a suffragette, let alone my suffering wife.
He did confess the NHS had fuck-all that could cope, with vacant geriatrics who ingest their flower-dope,

But still, he said, you're in good trim, as he scribbled out a note.

A prescription. "A waste of good Viagra…" was what the fucker wrote.

On my return, I found the Mrs, head stuck in a book.

"I've found out why it doesn't work," she said, "here, take a look…"

THE MIRACLE GRO-ERS GUIDE TO GROWING GIANTS FROM PLANTS AND SEEDS.

"That's why it's still so tiny! It doesn't work on weeds!"

Le Crevasse De Plombier

Le Crevasse de Plombier. The builder's crack.
Why do these tradesmen wear garments so slack?
Running up ladders, crawling on knees
With strides round their ankles by several degrees...
Sol the Brickie weighs in at twenty-two stone.
His trackie bottoms have a life of their own –
While Sol's on the trowel and pointing bricks up,
His labourer stands by, just to pull his Nicks up.
Rudi's the plumber who wears M & S shorts.
Except on a Sunday, when CK he sports.
But still in a size with a waistband so slack,
That even on Sundays he shows off his crack.
As hairy and sweaty as any bloke's bum
And not the one powdered by every bloke's Mum.
A sight not invited, and far from sublime
If you're trying to eat your lunch at the time.
The Champ of them all is Conor. A grafter.
A labourer. Shifts stuff. But his Joggers come after.
One rung up the ladder, they're one rung behind.
Seven rungs later, a full moon springs to mind.
At least Conor changes his knickers each day, to judge by his colourful drawers on display,
which prompts me to think that they're all like baboons,
but instead of red arses, we get pantaloons.

Swing round the scaffold; show off your credentials!
Make sure that the world sees your basic essentials!
And if Boss or Armani don't take 'em aback,
then give 'em the ultimate: Show 'em your crack!
Climb up the ladder, or crawl on all fours!
Make sure that the world gets full sight of your drawers!
Ecce Homo Erectus, in his own habitat!
Could it be as Neanderthal as that…?
Old-fashioned overalls, coats, dungarees, kicked out in favour of kecks round their knees. Braces and belts mere things of the past…
If you wannabe noticed, set your strides at Half-Mast.
Imagine if Churchill had urged us to fight
with full view of his bum-cheeks and pants in full sight.
What if John Glenn's "giant step for mankind" showed the view of an astronaut's hairy behind? Imagine if Nelson said, "Pull up me kecks," instead of calling the duty that England expects…
So come on you builders! Have respect for your craft.
Hoist up the mizzen; don't exhibit your Aft,
The stonemasons speak of the "All Seeing Eye", the divine one, who witnesses all that goes by.
If you're planning on heaven the day kingdom comes, stop showing your God and us folks your bare bums.

On Moving into a Mobile Home

"Aluminium Coffin" the Mrs christened it,
as the caravan deliverers positioned it.
Though a mobile home it might have been,
in her days before those better days seen,
(when a caravan in Rhyl was all the rage.)
Her peeling paintwork showed her age.
If she only could talk, our aluminium coffin,
of those packeted ready-meals, all polished off in her
Formica dinette: all the boil-in-bag rice, the Vesta beef
curries and Fray Bentos pies, Beef gravy granules and quick-
oven fries.
She'd be telling her tale with tears in her eyes…
A temporary mistress for dirty weekends
A home-from-home holiday fostered to friends
or anyone up for a brief getaway
with misted-up views over Liverpool Bay
plus views of the neighbours to left and to right, out front
and out back, and the fence round the site.
Her en-suite facilities all fully appointed
for midgets or dwarves or acute double-jointed,
though normal-sized persons ablute at the risk
of at least a black eye, or at worst a slipped disc.
Carrera white marble in a faux-tiled sheet with real plastic
fittings and wood-effect seat.

Her oak-veneer cupboards and arses-out drawers with odd-sets of cutlery and dog-eared jigsaws, the dominoes, board games all missing a bit and kites tangled up with the badminton kit, our washed-up sarcophagus oozes the stuff of home-from-home comfort while living it rough.

The aluminium coffin is now laid to rest;
Just one more off-season, or six months at best… Plumbed in, wired up, her lights flicker aglow, all Calor-gassed up with the hob on the go,
the kettle's soon whistling, and one for the pot! It might be home comfort, but home it is NOT.

How to Write a Folk-Song If You Can't Play an Instrument

If you want to write a folk-song, stick your finger in your ear
You'll wonder what the fuck it does, but your voice comes out right queer.
Then strip off bollock-naked, and skip around the park –
hugging trees and bushes, but sod the Holly for a lark...
Summer is y'comen in, yeah singeth out ye cuckoo Oaken coal de-baggy-ed be, up-ended on t't barbecoo
Blow away the morning dew, the dew, and the dew
I left the sunroof open and the fucking seat's wet through.
So now you're back to nature, with your balls like frozen peas. Drink fifteen pints of heavy ale, and start to think of these;
Tragedies. Slavery. The girl who broke your heart –
or the time you shat your Sunday kecks, when you only meant to fart.
Oh, the ship went down with the captain, as we fired the distress rocket. And pity it was the bastard drowned, with the kitty in his pocket.
Oh, my love gave me a thorn-ed rose, that pricked her little finger, green did grow the gangrene-o, so serve her right, the minger.
Agony, despair, and toil: The plight of the working man.
Ships going down. Mines collapsing. Any shit, or fan.

Or quoth the English countryside – the darling buds of May,
with a Hey-Nonny-No and a Fal-di-Lah, and a hint of Doris Day.
All hail ye Cornish ploughmen, for the fields are ripe for sickle!
Ploughmans Lunch £4.95. Extra for the pickle.
Ol' Yeller was the finest sheepdog that the Dales did ever clap eyes on.
I thought the tin held dogfood-tripe but the label did read pizen.
Grow a beard and drink another fifteen pints of ale.
Pick a subject: Pick your voice, and go on – tell your tale!
Chuck in some hint of humour – regardless of the plight –
A good folk song will always find a diamond in the shite.
Oh, hurry-urry up fair maiden, for marry-ed we shall be!
So she slid right down the banister, and warmed me up my tea.
For fifteen score five years & ten, o'er mountain, moor,
and crag & glen they plodded on, these weary men.
They'll never trust Sat-Nav again.
Now buy yourself a tambourine. There's no need for a tune.
Your voice somewhere twixt snoring, and howling at the moon,
Just bellow out your round-de-lay, your ballad, or your sonnet,
And tap your feet in time as if your life depended on it.
In eighteen-hundred and seventy-six, (tap-tap) *we sailed the seven seas.*
bound beyond where dragons dwell, to the land of mushy peas.
…and I be just a minstrel-boy (rattle tambourine) *who readeth,*
writeth none, but whosoever counteth seas? I only counted one.
…and sing the bugger up out loud: as if you speak the truth,
and if your words should harbour doubt, howl "Christ" or
"yea, foresooth" …just look pained, into the distance, while
you trill the tambourine,
and sing fuck-all, as if the silence paints some ghastly scene.

…and gone she was, forever, just a shadow in the mist…
(tambourine trill; silence, still)
I didn't put the handbrake on - I parked her when I's pissed.
Or: *And should you ever doubt me boys, then let me tell thee true, for sure as Christ was crucified, and knackers have I two –*
Then take my word, and let thee heed, and save a sorry dance – Never trust a man who tucks his shirt into his pants.
So now, you minstrel wannabe, I leave to your devices
Buy yourself some sandals, and don't eat bread in slices.
Save the whale, save the planet, save your fucking breath.
Those wailing fucking folk-singers will be my fucking death.

My Mrs.?

My Mrs has Alzheimers.
Dementia... And some.
Sometimes she's my sister.
Sometimes she's my mum.
At three O'clock this morning,
She was ready for The Ball.
In evening dress and opera-purse,
Her mother's pearls, and all.
I drove her twice around the block
(It's easier than dramas)
The dashboard clock said four o'clock,
when she noticed my pyjamas.
We must go home! She tucked me in,
and brushed me on the cheek.
Whatever world she's living in,
It's different every week.
A visit to the Village Inn:
Our local hostelry.
But not the same one I was in:
She asked for her Room-key.
She's still my Mrs Still a Mum.
Still the Grandkids' Nana,
my bemused, familiar house-guest
since dementia overran her.
Still the girl who blessed my life,

When we plied our troth together.
Still the lass I took as wife
Come foul wind or fair weather.
Still the girl, if fate had thrown
Dementia's curse on me,
would keep me as her very own.
As ever, selflessly.
So if I'm not her dashing Beau,
But some other, in her eyes,
Or just the grumpy so-and-so…
I'll go on, in disguise
and relish in the moment when
Our eyes might meet as one,
And we laugh together, once again…
No matter so soon gone.
A radio tune. A baby's cry,
might prompt us back in sync.
For just one second: eye to eye.
Then gone, in a blink.
I'll not desert my precious lass —
Whoever she might be.
I'll long that the song of a nightingale
might bring her back to me.

Make My Day

Should you ever meet the Bailiffs at your door one early morn, pour the blokes a cup of tea before you pour on scorn.
Or should you have a tax collector eyeing up your worth, pay him the dues befitting any dweller of this earth.
Ticket written; traffic wardens will not change their mind.
Underneath the uniforms, we're all one of a kind.
And should the rude receptionist not open up your doors,
She might be struggling for a smile; in which case, give her yours!
Or maybe, you should simply kick the Bailiff in the 'taters,
The pond-life dwelling, bowler-hatted callous masturbators.
Any tax-collector's worthy of a painful Glasgow greeting;
Nut the fucker. Casualty can take the minutes of the meeting. The parking-ticket on your screen, one inevitable destination – the traffic-warden's arsehole, with crushed glass for lubrication.

The stroppy-cow receptionist might claim it's just her job,
but does the door get opened when she's been smacked in the gob?
Take deep breaths, they tell us. Count from one to ten...
Like Rocky on the canvas... at nine, spring up again?
Do we turn the other cheek, or just roll with the punch?
Smack the twat between the eyes, or take him out to lunch?

Two wrongs don't make a right. 'Tis true, but we know all along... The wronged one isn't always right, the righteous often wrong... but when ill-met with a Jobsworth who takes it to the letter,
who could deny if you blacked their eye, you'd feel a damn sight better?
Whatever you inherited, can you say it's 'cos you're meek?
or when a slap is merited, can you turn the other cheek?
Do you demand a bloody eye, now you're single-sighted?
Is it worth you pulling teeth, because your smile's been blighted?
Your antagonist's fate, and yours beyond, is always up to you. For your own good sake, bake 'em a cake. Matthew (5:38-42). They'll still be wankers, one and all. But they'll be bang to rights - when your heads upon the pillow.
And them not sleeping nights.

Other Search Engines Are Available

There was a time not long ago, when all I said was true.

At least my words were taken so, when e'er she sought my view... But since she got her iPad, every answer gets cross-checked.
No longer I'm her Canny Lad; my words are now suspect.
Google it.
Who's that bloke, stood by John Wayne? Whiskers, no teeth?
"Walter Houston!" I explain, assured of my belief...
"No it isn't! Take a look!" On her iPad, she displays
the cast, the film, the crew, the book. "I told you, Gabby Hayes!" Google it.
She asks, "*Is* so 'n' so dead...?" But before I've an answer, She's googled it. Five years ago. Lost to bowel cancer. I'm still racking my brains as to who he might be – While she's reading out his whole biography.
Google it.
I've just boiled her eggs, with her soldiers in line... When She questions the perfect soft-boiled cooking time but before I protest, that they're timed to the second,
it seems dippy-eggs take less time that I'd reckoned.
Google it.
...so the bullet-hard chooks are completely my fault, my cookery books to be taken with salt...

The Font of all knowledge dethroned off his perch;
The genius from college? Not according to "Search."
Google it.
My credentials now tainted, drag/dropped to the Trash. The window-frame painted, gets searched Forward/Hash. No matter explanation, that the window-frame is rotten –
I get How-It's-Done on YouTube, my opinion forgotten.
Google it.
"You should have done this. You should have done that." Used to be MY lines. Before some daft twat invented the iPad. Instant access to media. I'm now married to an encyclopaedia.
Google it.

The Companionship Years

It used to be "just do it!" Dive in head first, the norm!
Now we must review it, maybe check the water's warm –
and even that seems ages since; somewhere, doubt appeared.
Crept up and stole those instincts, like a slowly greying beard.
We once held hands for joy. We hold them still, though not
to cling together, girl and boy, not waste the time we've got,
but now the hand is ever there, and reaching in the dark –
not stepping stones across a weir, to a picnic in the park,
the gleam within her eye, as then, still sweet sixteen to me,
yet sparkles for whatever's aye her ill mind's eye might see…
for which I'd settle anyhow; no crystal chandeliers
but dancing still, we'd take a bow! Two faltering old dears.
The bodies we once worshipped, given way to wear and tear
to behold a whole new fellowship, as if the scars weren't there,
though open wounds appearing yet:
encountering every day as if the time our eyes first met,
now blinkered with dismay…
"Just do it!" Oh, as if we could. Dive in head first again?
…dismiss the picnic? Yes I would, I'd strip off all, but then
We used to… oh, "we used to" dwells forever in my mind,
with her sunny spells just greying cells, her body left behind -
Her eyes, her neck, her lips, her curls; but a new girl every
day. All-sparkling in their mother's pearls; I wish that one

might stay on each occasion when some spark
might bring us in as one, jump right in? Here in the dark?
Together? Long, long gone.
Tomorrow, while the stepping-stones be taken on my own,
I'll clasp her hand, her ringed bones, and know a love full-blown,
And treasure every instant when my girl might catch my eye,
And we'll skip up to the picnic, as companionship rolls by.

Mole Madness

There are manicured lawns and then there is mine:
There's nowt wrong with moss, and the daisies are fine.
A billiard-table it never will be, especially with the odd dog-turd or three.
So when I espied a neat-piled soil pyramid
'midst the moss and the daisies, guess what muggins 'ere did.
I welcomed the mole and his wife to my lawn… unaware of
the groundworks the bastards would spawn.
Within days my embracing of wild-life was gone;
Instead of the daises and dogmuck, read "Somme" –
As in World War One at its muddiest worst,
It looked like the whole fucking lawn had just burst.
Molehills everywhere. No square yard escaped.
Complete devastation. My lawn had been raped.
Neat piles of topsoil all over my plot,
Leaving hardly a space for the poor dog to squat.
Four hills filled a 'barrow, and ten barrows shifted, a half-ton
of topsoil the bastards had lifted!
…and come the next morning, it's back to square one!
A half-ton of topsoil… It went on and on.
The topsoil I'd spreaded all over my veg
had got to a slag-heap as high as the hedge,
While the lawn slowly sank by a mole's width a week, I was
losing my land by the pound, so to speak!
…and losing my patience as remedies failed; the more I

upset him, the more hills prevailed. Apparently, moles have a dislike for hair... ...and coffee, tobacco, and cat-shit (I swear!)
...each mole-hated substance got stuffed down the holes but far from discourage, encouraged more moles.
A sonic deterrent, with a battery-powered Shoo! Seemed tuned to a station the moles listened to...
...and the traps all failed miserably, gave 'em some sport. A hundred times set, not one single mole caught.
And at first, I confess I'd have dreaded the sight, but I'd happily club one to death now all right.
There are people who think that a mole's cute and cuddlesome, an underground teddy-bear, nowt more than troublesome. Well, listen you wankers, they're fucking well NOT.
Just wait 'til the fuckers have chewed up your plot.
They're muscle-bound monsters with shovels for hands.

Each nail hard as tungsten: their teeth, jagged fangs.
They can shovel through rubble like a miner from Swansea
Like a J C B in a black velvet Onesie.
They're not fucking blind. They just like the dark;
They've got thermal night-vision, play blind for a lark,
So that if any wriggling morsel comes inner...
The white cane gets chucked and he'll have it for dinner.
They're tunnelling around right under our soles, ready to drag us down into their holes
And gobble us up with the slugs and the lice.
They can smell us a mile off, which ain't very nice.
'cos they follow me round when I'm out on the bit where they've left me some grass,

and the dog is scared to shit.
I can hear the moles scratching, all circling around
'till they rip at my bootlace, drag me underground…
There's a man in a white coat who says he's my friend.
He says he can take me to where this will end,
Free from the monsters who've made my life hell.
A mole-free enclosure. It's padded, as well.

Signs of Life

Planet K218B
has signs of life, apparently.
A sun like ours, and rivers, too.
Some bits green, and others, blue.
Life on K218B
could be no more than sub-algae;
Ingredients yet to be ignited.
And yet it gets us all excited.
Meanwhile, here on planet three
We treat our life disgracefully.
Burn the climate! Choke the seas!
Kill each other! Chop the trees!
I wonder how long will it be?
before Planet K218B
gets a visit from our mother ship,
and turned into a rubbish-tip.
There was a time when planet three resembled K218B
A billion years ago, as pure.
Evolution? Not so sure.

"...and there's a real buzz about the ground here at Lords..."

On the ultimate day of the final Test, and The Ashes stood two-all.
We'd had our tea and the stumps were set for a contest ball-by-ball.

Grandad was the Aussies, and I played Englands' best —
Not this years' team — but Wisden's cream — like Botham and the rest.

Grandad was Don Bradman — and I was Flintoff, up for owt.
Out to get the great man, my grandad, who could clout.

No fielding from the rose-beds, or even worse, next door —
I'd bowl him straight, I reckoned: Don Bradman, out, no score.

But as I paced the run-up, there hanging from the tree
I saw a buzzing wasp's nest — in the line of my googly.

Bradman, who had farted, was waving with the bat —
Grandad! Wasp's nest! Bradman said, "I'll soon get rid of that."

Grandad summoned Hercules, his trusted upright bike,

and whittled at the clothes-prop end to make a jousting-spike.

With a bucket for a helmet, and a gasmask on his face,
he pedalled like Sir Lancelot at a good Lance Armstrong pace.

The jousting pole was way off shot, but the bucket hit the nest,
so Grandad kept on pedalling – a blur of shorts and vest.

The lance became a pole-vault pole as it dug into the lawn
As Grandad out-flew all the wasps, Sir Lance-aloft, airborne.

He landed in the compost-heap, and came out fighting mad
– "We'll have our game of cricket! We'll fix the buggers, lad!"

Out came his trusty catapult – the one he used for cats,
who shat amongst his flower-beds instead of catching rats.

With one eye closed like Popeye, and some good old Grandad swearing,
and a good old British-made 15/16ths ball-bearing.

Grandad let fly. And didn't it just. Pure hell in just one aim.
Straight through the blasted greenhouse – and next door's cucumber-frame.

"Bradman returns to the pavilion," – called Grandad from his shed,
With a scheme of wasp-oblivion buzzing in the great man's head.

He soon emerged with a fishing-rod, and a paraffin blow-torch.
"Sit back and watch the fireworks, lad – I've a tree-wasp's arse to scorch."

The blow-torch dangled, spitting fire, at the end of a cane carp-pole
And lit the leaves, the branch, the tree, but not a wasp's arse-hole.

Instead, the flaming Catherine-wheel burnt all within its orbit,
including Grandad's cane Carp-pole, but Grandad just ignored it...

...screaming hell, and death, profanities (and an involuntary Grandad's fart) he thrust his flaming bayonet right through the wasp's nest's heart.
I ran. And Grandad ran. By God, could Grandad fly! and from the Lord's Pavilion we watched the bastards die.

Full play resumed. The wicket cleared, and Bradman's looking worn.
His face red-burnt: his knuckles barked, and the arse of his shorts all torn,

But nevertheless, there's a steely glint in Grandad's wrinkled eye
As he waits for Flintoff's run-up from the end by the old pigsty.

A Yorker! Blast! The stinker! He hadn't bargained that,
and before old Grandad blinked, the bugger went beneath
the bat.

The stumps well split, the crowd went wild and Flintoff
celebrated.
And the Ashes? Just a blackened ball of charcoal-wasps
cremated.

My Ol' Fergie Does That...

There's a rich kid 'as neighbours my furtherest field, An' E farms it as if one of us.
'E 'as this hequipment with c'mputers 'n that, with one tractor, the soize of a bus.
I seed 'im out walkin' with two queer dogs
Whoile I was out getting' up beet,
'an as I hello'd 'im, his tractor went past
with no bugger sat in the seat!
I shuts off the Fergie, 'an 'Im I surveys
in 'is moleskin coat 'n' posh wellies
'n' I says to 'Im, "Ow do you drive it?"
'n' 'E says, "I just watch it on tellies!"
"My grey Fergie does that!" I tel't 'im
an' dropped the old girl into second.
Dropped in the rake, 'n' put her on idle,
Jumped out of the seat an' 'Im beckoned,
"Jus' watch that ol' Fergie go off on her own, As straight an' as true as I'd do.
I'll catch'r up in a minute; no time for the telly. She cost eight hundred quid when bran' new..."
Well! The toff was really right put out,
'is million dollar tractor offended.
By the time I'd recovered my Fergie,
I'd a good show of beets all up-ended.
But the Toff was up for a showdown –

An' 'E tells me it saves 'im such time.
"Time to do what?" I am askin'
'n' 'E tells me, "For work." What a crime.
So I turns roun' and tells 'im quite truly,
"My ol' grey Fergie does that!
While I'm sat in 'er saddle I sorts it all out,
'n' my hoffice is under my 'at."
Well, "E went gabblin' on about satellites
And Nav-Sat that tells where she's at,
'n' them meteorological sensors…"
Oi tel't I'm. "My Fergie does that!"
It's a poor man that doesn't know where he might be when
'is arse is parked firm in the seat,
'n' by God I'm damn sure if her bonnet is wet, then it's
rainin' so bugger the wheat!

I seen your machine at the County Show
Where they let poor farmers loike me
Climb up in the cab, 'n' 'ave a go
'n' I daredly believed it, bless me!
Hair conditionin'! My ol' Fergie's got that;
But the diff'rence between yours 'n' mine,
Is that your hair conditionin's by thermostat,
Whereas mine comes from 'is good self; divine.
The full-swivel harmchair I'd loike by my telly but as comfy
she is, you can keep.
If I 'ad such as half a brown ale in my belly
I'd be always fallin' asleep!
'n that radio 'n four-speaker stereo,
'n the Bluetooth, whatever, complete –
if you're getting' computers to drive it

just why did they put in a seat?
My Ol Grey Fergie, God bless her –
Does everythin' yours does, with class –
She'll not make forty unless it's downhill
And a trailer of grain up her arse
I've a ploughshare fer this 'n another for that 'n the drills 'n the discs 'n all told,
there's a harrow and bailer,
The fence-postin' piler
A full tippin' trailer
The mower and flailer
my 'ome made boom sprayer
'n' the bench saw, all sixty years old.
I bought 'er brand new at two guineas a week,
Includin' the 'ol bleedin' kit.
She came with one spanner, 'an turns on a tanner in places your bugger won't fit!"
but our Gentleman was'n a-lis'nin' at all
'E wuz scratchin' his head through 'is 'at.
Fer 'is magic machine 'ad gone into a stall
'n' 'is phone said her battery was flat.
"My ol' Fergie does that!" I says to the Prat
an' I know that she can't hold a candle
to your on-board computer 'n' Nav-Sat 'n' that, but she'll start with one crank of the 'andle!

Extract from P.C. McTavish's Evidence
H.M. Ministry of Defence v Grampian Police

"Mah name is Jock McTavish –Ah'm a Po-lisMan throo 'n throo, but there's nae much craic on the bare tarmac of the B8152.
We'd a sheep on the loose, 'n' the shepherder's hoose wis a mile o'er mountain and glen. Ah wis aal on ma lonesome, 'n the boredom had grown some,
Tae the de'il's own mischief, ye ken?
Ah had a wee speed-gun in mah kit – Darth Vader wid be proud o' it.
Yir actual speed, digitally decreed... Ah wis tryin' tae speed-check a blue-tit.
It wid hardly but strain tae record, ascertain the speed o' the traffic roond there; them the sheep didnae slow doon, yi'd ne'er put yir toe doon,
wi' the cattle-grids everywhere!
Bit a whoosh! And a Bang! Mah ears did harangue, as a Fighter-Jet flew thru yon Peaks. Here 'n' gone in a second.
The tissue-box beckoned –
Ah reckoned ah'd shat in mah breeks.
The Fockers were flyin' where walkers were vy-in' for airspace along wi' aircrew. Knocked' a climber's hat skewiff!
Yi'd forgive th' air-crew if
yon wing hit a climber or two.
'n' gone jist as quick! Jist a vapour-trail slick, and a silence

that rattled mah ears.
Then a bluidy great WHACK! The bugger wis back.
His photo wis worth a few beers...
Ah went from boredom tae fuckin' Flash Gordon, 'n' got him smack-dab in mah sights.
Ah praised indeed, mah squary bead, and got him bang tae rights.
Eight-hundred 'n' eighty miles 'n' hoor he clocked, when he shuid hae kept tae fifty! Ah checked mah ray-gun, chuffed 'n' shocked. Yon speed-gun's pretty nifty.
Afoor ah've turned mah heid tae see, another fucker aims at me, 'n' clippin' tops off trees! Yon pilot shrugs his heid at me, as if in an apology, 'n' ah'm knockin at the knees.
His co-ordinates wir locking in, as rails lock in on trains, an E-lectronic heid the ba', wi' chips fir fuckin' brains 'n' all of NATO's armoury had locked on tae the enemy, a cunt wi' radar just like me, a hostile cunt wi' no I.D.
The fucker's Battle-Station had but one set destination – the beggar wi' the gun!
Mah Po-lisMan's intuition said, Ah only had one mission, that's tae hoik yir kilt 'n' RUN!
Ye'd never learn the three-point turn ah turned that fuckin' Panda. Took out the drystone dykes 'n' all, tae scared tae tak a gander – Bit in mah flight Ah kept a-sight within mah rear-view mirror Tae see that fuckin' missile getting' nearer, fuckin' nearer.
Ah revved that knackered Escort like a fuckin' Black 'n' Decker! Nae race had pace wid e'er disgrace oor windin' neck 'n' necker! The fucking thing wis on mah airse, roond every bend tae toon. Ah ducked intae the car-wash – and whacked in half-a-croon.

Ah thought ah'd lost it, instead ah'd washed it, the missile on me still!
A nuclear spit 'n' polish, fuck! And ah had paid the bill.
The war-heid knew its stuff a'right – it knew it's highway code.
It ne'er used a bus-lane, and ne'er left the road,
but kept wi'in a legal speed, and even flashed its lights
for the bairns tae fetch their fitba'. It fair gave me the shites...
Ah nipped in tae the drover's arms, tae fortify wi' dram and the bugger hovered on ma tail – Ah yelled at it tae scram, and raised mah boot in anger, took a swing tae kick it
so whin the warheid growled at me, Ah gi' the cunt a ticket.
The bluidy thing took on a hum, like a blind upholsterer's thumb its pointed heid a-shinin' red, like a boil on a gibbon's bum.
'n' then an angry tickin' started, accompanied by growls, A-tickin' from within. Ah farted. The growls were from mah bowels.
Ah took the road back to the hills from whence the beggar came, to see if ah could lose it, and get mahsel' off hame
Ah slipped the clutch like Starsky and Hutch, 'n hit that fuckin' pedal.
If ah got haim late, wi' mah new-found mate, ah'd need a fuckin' medal.
If mah old trusty panda clocked a hundred mile an hour
the missile clocked at ninety-nine... (point) milliseconds slower.
When e'er ah turned, the missile turned, and braked whin ah braked too.
Ah tell this court, Ah wis distraught, Ah kenned not whit tae

do.
Then, on mah right, came intae sight, MacDougall's farm's dung-heap.
A reekin' rottin' pile o' shite that made his neighbours weep.
A railway-sleeper'd bay o' shite, nae thermo-nuclear dump, but nature's best that comes, egest from good auld Scottish rump.
Ah aimed for it. Ah smelled the shit. 'n then ah fuckin jumped for it.
The Panda, the missile, straight intae the shit-pile, Ah'd scored a direct hit.
Nae nuclear violence, but cow-shit 'n' silence, nae hometown turned intae Ground Zero No' wiped off the map, as ah wiped off the crap, no' dead as a door-nail, a Hero!
Mah name is Jock McTavish, a Polis-Man, throo 'n' throo, there's none o' this is bullshit!" except McDougall's coo-shit, ah tell ye, it's all true.

"Jock" is an amalgam of two true stories: in 1999, a traffic cop did in fact let curiosity get the better of him, and pointed a radar speed gun at a jet fighter on manouvres, with the consequences that the machine's autopilot switched to battle-stations. In the 60's, during submarine trials in the Inner Hebrides, an old Royal Navy man assures me he saw a torpedo rocket go up the beach, turned hard a-starboard up the coast road and destroyed a Triumph Herald ticking over while the owner was posting a letter. Too good to resist!

On-Line / Off-line / Life-line

Super-stud studies his lap-top
Bed-sit and rat-shit's his back-drop.
On-line it's a penthouse in Chelsea,
The driver Dimitri, the housekeeper Elsie.
A mountain of mail in his in-box.
He's in three-day-old Y-fronts and bed-socks.
On-line it's all pin-striped Armani,
The office in Soho, the lunch Giovanni.
Macho-man maintains his profile.
A barrel of lard and immobile.
On-line it's all jogging and tennis,
the trainers are Nike, the squash-partner Dennis.
He's got beautiful friends on his face-book.
and the benefit-fraud on his case-book.
On-line he's pursuing Candida,
A professional dancer, a part-time cheer-leader.
Candida has lots of admirers.
She gives them her love, and her virus.
On-line it's up-close and yours only.
The condo with sea view, this occupant lonely.
Cheer-leader studies her lap-top.
A pimp and spent needles her back-drop.
On-line she just curses her agent,
The sign-off abrupt; the agent impatient!
Candida snatches a minute.

Her in-box has super-stud in it:
On-line she says, "Desperate to rumba."
Her hope, a free ticket. He just wants her number.
Super-stud eats from the carton.
He's got porno on-screen, and a hard-on.
On-line they small-talk up their romance.
He sees them screwing. She sees a slow-dance.
The chorus-girl sleeps in her vomit.
Her Qwerty's a tourniquet on it.
On-line they both end with a smiley.
She dreaming of Redford; he dreaming of Kylie.

1 out of 10 cats?

If the cat brought in a Tuna,
I'd be happy to concede
That the flavour of her catfood
Fulfils her every need.
If the cat was shot for rustling
the odd sheep or straying cow,
I'd accept her cat-food's natural
And simply wonder how?
And...
If salmon is the choice of cats,
(especially in gravy)
I'd reckon our adopted cat
Was rescued from the Navy.
I doubt our cat could catch a duck,
never mind a turkey.
But the packet says, "Her natural choice."
A claim that's nought but quirky...
not vegetables, for a start!
Carrots, peas, in jelly?
Have you ever smelled a moggy-fart?
Like an open sewer in Dheli.
No wonder, when her chosen food
Is a mouse-head's crack and crunch.
The heart ripped from a throbbing wren
makes OUR cat's perfect lunch.

Spider-flavour might be good.
With moths to add nutrition.
In bacon-fat, licked from the pan,
is what they should be dishin'.
Or Field-Vole-mousse with rye-grass?
Braised Bluetit's brains in cream?
And don't forget the Weetabix.
Rice pudding's our cat's dream.
Mouse-flavour seems too obvious.
But why not RAT-atouille?
Or Squirrel-livers au Fois Gras?
So much more Mew-Mew-Mew-y!
Our cat was clearly not brought up
To catch Atlantic Prawns.
Pacific Tuna as out of grasp
As a leather-clad beast with horns.
"Juicy flaked beef and veg," so it says,
and I long for the day when our cat
drops a two-ton Aberdeen Angus
with its throat ripped out, on the mat.

If the Bard Were Alive Today

If William Shakespeare walked the streets
In his hosiery and lace
Just load him up with leaflets
And he'd not look out of place.
What would he make of Stratford?
Still living off his name,
Four hundred years after
He quit the writing game?
A turnstile at his garden gate
With selfies on the lawn
The tourists circumnavigate
the house where he was born.
The carpark at his in-laws place
Enough for twenty buses.
If William Shakespeare showed his face,
He'd wonder what the fuss is.
Should Will engage the plate-glass doors
of the centre in his name,
he'd be bewildered he's the source
of Stratford's claim to fame.
The gift-shops and the souvenirs
Might prompt a puzzled shrug,
But he'd surely like a tea-towel
Or a William Shakespeare mug.
If William Shakespeare did appear

He'd be well pleased to see
His plays still staged here year on year
At ye good olde R S C.
He'd see his works were still in print –
Hardbound, audio. Tablet.
A comic-book Othello
The Graphic Novel! Hamlet!
...and wonder where his royalties went
His merchandising rights
He'd have the town of Stratford
Within Ye Lawyer's sights.
"My balded head! A brand well–bred,
in tragedy or Sonnet.
So glad to see that I'm not dead!
My agent is upon it."

Bogseat Blues

I write in praise of soft-close. (As in soft-close toilet seat)
'cos, as far as urination goes for a bloke it's hard to beat.
Whoever put in the gizmo
That descends it like a leaf
I declare a national hero
When e'er I take relief.
But the seat in our downstairs bog
Is a man-hating guillotine,
Drops like a chain-sawn rotten log
Unannounced, and twice as mean.
Sometimes it's fine, and stands up straight
Like all good bog-seats do.
I un-zip. Lift the seat; and wait…
but it's always when mid-through…
The Whack! Won't chop my dick off
It'll never crush my balls
But every time it happens
There's piss on all three walls.
And on my shoes. And on the seat
(that's the seat no longer upright.
The seat that's gone full ninety degrees
And flicked my dick in flight.)
Or panicked me to squeeze the end
to try and stop mid-stream.
Or twist the end to a double-bend

to aim it where I mean.
Either way, the seat has dropped:
A milli-micro-second tops!
An ablutive exercise half-cropped
…now, just mop up all the slops.
but the bog-seat has the final call,
When we're all done and cleaned up
And the Mrs screaming down the hall,
"You've left the bloody seat up!"

A Winter's Tale

There're people that swear by the caravan life, but this don't include me, and don't ask the wife. "For better or worse" gets kicked into touch when sharing a caravan the size of a hutch.
The toilet's a tannoy, there's no quiet cack. The lid won't stay up, so I piss out the back. The walls are so thin that a fart passes through with no loss of volume, nor noxious-ness too.
At least we're not shagging – perish the thought that anyone passing would know of our sport: For our bedroom's the width of a telephone box. I can lie down full length, if I'm not wearing socks.
The kitchen's got everything: every known germ.
The real-oak veneers got real-oak wood worm
A wall-to wall, generous, five foot six wide.
But swing a cat? No. Well, not our cat – I've tried.
And the cooker's gas-marks might go up to eight but whatever the dial says, it's set to "cremate". The grill spits a fireball that takes off your face but can't warm the blood of your average plaice,
When turned up full throttle, it gives up the ghost – a week to grill crumpets, two weeks for toast.
But we don't use it much. It takes three men to light it.
One turning knobs. One to pile sandbags. One to ignite it.
Cupboards a-plenty, but of sweet fuck-all use,

we're stowing the cornflakes and Rice Crispies loose.
We've got fitted wardrobes, but not fit to please, while the sock-draws are ample for most amputees.
The velvet upholstery lost all of its opulence –
having soaked up some forty-odd seasons of flatulence.
The farts laid to rest in the festering foam,
that no parasite, bed-bug or flea would call home.
But it's cosy enough when the gas-fires on full – the carbon monoxide quite palatable, compared with the oxygen coming in neat
from the draught round your ear'oles, the draught round your feet...
Panoramic bay-windows, the sheet-glass as thin
as the clingfilm your mum wraps your sandwiches in.
Thermally as good as the skin of a trout,
i.e. keep the cold in, and let the warm out.
Overcoat, thermal gloves, scarf, woolly hat;
just to watch telly. And that's just the cat.
The 'van's central heating only extends
to sucking on mints and fisherman's friends.
One day they might find us deep-frozen in bed like two Birdseye haddocks, or maybe instead they will find us in 'jama's all rosy, and pink with the CO1 gas-alarm gone on the blink.
Or maybe we'll live, and can wave her goodbye
To the caravan graveyard up in the sky.
Dragging her arse as they cart her away,
With only the rust-marks to tell of her stay.

Kids of Today...

The rugby balls in *my* day, lad, were made of bloody leather
A bladder stitched, with laces in, to hold it all together.
The ones today have adverts on, in supersonic plastic;
They'll reach the sticks from miles away, toe-poked by any spastic.
The boots we wore were leather, too – wi' toecaps like a brick. We dubbin'd 'em to last for years, the leather was that thick. But now they buy 'em twice a year, at sixty quid a throw, like ballet-shoes, all soft and pink, wi' fuck-all on the toe.
...and we *invented* tie-ups. *Our* socks were made of wool.
Hung around your ankles, they'd hold a gallon each, half-full.
So we tied 'em up. Or taped 'em up. Either way, no fuss.
Bryan Habana in woolly socks? He couldn't catch a bus.
We didn't have post-protectors, like cushions in a pram.
What rugby-post can do you harm? An advertising scam.
And kicking tees. Kicking tees! With some so high, at that, you could HEAD the pill between the posts, that's any spawny twat...
...And if the ref should send you off, he didn't need a card.
We didn't remonstrate at all – we'd make him drink a yard.
But now you get your yellow card – Ooh! Naughty boy! Smacked wrist!
Ten minutes off? Within the game? I'd come back on half-pissed!

And nowadays, if you should burst a pimple on your head, you can have a blood-replacement – your mate comes on instead!
And half-a-Guinness later, or a few more, with a shout –
Your mate comes off; you go on; what the fuck's *that* all about?
Gum-shields. Body armour. Like that American football farce.
And passive scrums. Passive scrums? You can shove 'em up your arse.
What we want is what we played – that's eighty-minutes' worth
of rugby – Rugby Union – the greatest game on earth.
At that, my son, I'll take "Time out" (*another* innovation!)
And summon up my aches and pains to find some inspiration.
We weren't allowed a substitute: we turned out fifteen men!
A fucked-up shoulder, a broken nose; we went back on again!
And every time the cold wind blows, and crippled with arthritis,
We curse the wounds of long ago that come back now to bite us.
We made a try: we saved a try: we played on, through the pain –
And crippled, cursing, bleeding – we *loved* the fucking game.

A Fen End Foursome

You can't beat three sets of tennis, with a four of misfit blokes,
No lightning serve to menace.
No super-spin ground strokes.
Those players on the telly
With a back-hand like a whip
Don't have a beer-belly
Or a knee that gives 'em jip.
You might get dodgy line-calls,
You won't hear screams or grunts
You'll not hear calls for new balls
Just the gasps from clapped-out codgers
(whatever rhymes with "grunts" ?)
There's no appeals for foot-faults, Or apologies for "nets",
The scathing wit and insults Is as good as tennis gets.
A mad dog prowls the chain-link and tries to eat each ball.
Nowt wrong with that, you might think but he eats the fence and all.
The yips and dodgy kick-ups are a feature of the court –
No need for Hawkeye's hiccoughs when the "trenches" have their sport...
You can't beat a Fen End foursome when old Briscoe's got his chores. A break to put Lou's supper on, or the loading of a horse...
When we'll soak in dappled sunlight falling over Georgian

bricks,
Just sit and put the world to rights. And at the same time take the piss.
We will pause and catch the songbirds, or the calling of the lark,
we will thrill to twilight's blackbirds rallying with us, towards the dark
or we'll stop and all stare upwards at the screaming 737's
as the 7:45 from God-knows-where comes landing from the heavens.
You can't beat a Fen End foursome
Where a cold beer's e'er on tap.
The setting pretty awesome
The standard pretty... crap.
But we have some right old knock-ups with long rallies doomed to end
in some great almighty cock-up – When the wood becomes your friend,
It's win-or-lose trench warfare, So a netcord, wood, so what?
When the ball zips up from nowhere, we all know it's hit the spot.
And every point applauded, no matter how it's won
A double fault net-corded is just tough luck, old son.
Competitive? Oh, yes. Not half. Despite arthritic joints
Clive's dodgy back just gets a laugh when faced with three match-points
So come final set, match point at last and like a dog that's seen the bone, Clive's up to serve. What's that he's heard?
Mrs Briscoe on the phone...
Oh, I couldn't miss a summer's eve nor November in the damp

when you're wiping snot upon your sleeve or hobbling with the cramp
'cos a Fen End tennis foursome is as good throughout the year - whether winter, spring or autumn, it will end up with a beer,
When the winners will commiserate with their feet up, on the bench
It's not your fault you lost, old mate – You can blame that fucking trench.
It's not about the win, or loss, it's all about the sport.
Sport always wins. Who gives a toss? On a dodgy tennis court?

Hashtag Nativity

... imagine, when Jesus was born, if that stable was wired
for Wi-fi, Bluetooth and cable,
and the humblest Bethlehem hostelry
was last-minute booked with AirBnB.
Via Sat-nav the Wise Men came from afar
Their eyes on their mobiles (forget the star).
Gifts in brown packaging for the Messiah,
A Spotify app for the heavenly choir.
And while Mary's facebook gets thousands of views,
Herod's convinced that it isn't fake news.
"Iesus Nazarenus Rex Iudeorum,"
it says on his i-Tablet, on every forum.
There'd hardly be time to sing Silent Night before instant celebrity gained its full height, and the wonder matured over thirty-odd years cropped. Photo-shopped. Imoji tears.
Check out the carpenter dotcom user reviews rate his credit hashtag temple forward slash jews live podcast from Galilee! Raging storm calmed! or... 5,000 fed! MacDonalds alarmed...
Would Lazarus rise in a Facetime-booked slot? And would they believe in him? Most likely not. The parables, sermons that drew passers-by. A virtual experience in full C G I.
Imagine. 2,000 years wiser, if that stable... The World Wide Web, would only disable; distort every word. There is only one way,

and whosoever believeth… were there on the day.

Our most valuable blessing on earth is our time, and not time to save, but to spend, most sublime; the journey becomes our most precious birth right – and an infant cannot learn a world overnight.

My neighbour is you. Your neighbour is me.

And that's all there is to Christianity.

From Bethlehem to Antioch via God knows, whatever.

Life isn't an instant, while love lasts forever.

Lost at Sea

"I do like that painting," she says from her chair.
(A boat in a sunset, with storms in the air,
the mood overcast); "It's as if you were there." Then she
says, "Where'd it come from?"
I respond, in despair...
"You painted it."
I have a love for that painting, from the moment created.
I remember the storms that we both navigated,
And the twelve months it took her, while I simply waited,
For when palette was rested, the trestle vacated.
She painted it.
Since then, it's adorned every drawing-room, hall, of Manor
and cottage, each perfect wall
in our land-lubber's life, who bear the sea's call.
We have gazed on the scene, the freedom we knew,
...and THAT squall.
She painted it.
She painted that freedom. She painted that sea.
She painted the moment. So... beautifully,
then lived in the moment for twelve months, still free.
It hangs on the wall, and she likes it?
Fuck me –
She painted it!
I look at that painting, and my course is set there. She captures the swell and with brush-stroke, sea-air! As if

soaked in sea-brine, every oil-tipped-hair, makes the moment
eternal, for me: I swear.
She painted it!
So many moments we've lost to such weather;
That squall we survived not to odds, but together.
How can the Creator their creation then sever
from memory, moment, or the creator's
endeavour?
when...
She painted it?

Mcmarlboro Man and the Smoking Ban

Ye cannae beat a roll-up when y'r gasping fir a fag,
Fer they beat y'r stinkin' Marlboro's wi' every bonny drag.
Coolness-tipped, yon noncie tabs that c'mon oot a packet
'r on'y fir lassies, or a shirt-lifter, in his poofter smokin' jacket.
Ye cannae beat a roll-up when ye've rolled-off, off a shag,
One minute gaspin' ecstacy, then hankin' fae a drag…
Ye'll get nae satisfaction oot o' post-coital nico-gum,
or scratch 'n' sniff the nico-patch like ye scratch 'n' sniff yir bum.
'n' ye cannae beat a roll-up fir the bringin' on a shite.
Ah rolls one up each mornin' and the same last thing at night, 'n' mix it wi' a cup o' tea; 'n' sit doon wi' the paper.
…'n' tak' a shit most leisurely, 'n' the missus curse the vapour.
Ye cannae beat a roll-up when y'r playin' o' the darts, dominos, cribbage, billiards – or whi'tever in your parts; fir any man's activity is best in clouds o' smoke –
'n' a half-time fag in a fitba' match is a braw bricht masterstroke.
Ye cannae beat a roll-up: Ne'er mind for the cough, that brings up slimy oysters like a tumor that's gone off. The rack clears out yir eyebaws 'n' yir testicles as well,
As ye clutch 'em, hackin' frae yir guts as yir lungs tak' on the swell.

Och, ye cannae beat a roll-up 'n' that's a fuckin' fact.
'n' ah should know, with all the fuckin' coughin' freely hacked.
But ye cannae beat a roll-up 'n' a roll-up is mah choice;
It's taxes, no' the swirlin' smoke! that maks me lose my voice.
If ah've a fuckin' cancer then ah've paid for it ma'sen
'n' ah couldnae hae' gone private; fir the government, y'ken?
They've taxed me on yon Rizlas, the baccy and the tabs.
They'd tax yon fucking fingers too, if they wir' up for grabs…
…'n' since that fuckin' smokin' ban, we're all to smoke al fresco – Well, fuck 'em all – the pubs and all! I'll buy my drink frae Tesco, 'n' smoke at hame, ne'er mind the company's no' like it's doon the pub; but the barmaid disnae suck my cock, nor disnae cook the grub!
Ye cannae beat a roll-up 'n' ah think ah've made mah point.
Ah've got the message, NHS! - it's no' a fuckin' joint!
"SMOKING KILLS! DON'T LET YOUR CHILDREN BREATHE IN YOUR FOUL SMOKE," I do agree. They can buy their ayn, if it wisnae sich a joke.
Oh, Ye cannae beat a roll-up when ye're ere pissed off wi' life – when yi'r last quids on the next race, or yi'r buryin' the wife. Or even in those moments, wi' your best mate in yi'r hand, Ye cannae beat a roll-up. Shit. Yi'r ne'er aloon wi' a Strand.

Santa's Visit

T'was Christmas Eve at the Salvage Yard, and the snow was falling thick. A glistening snow-white blanket covered flagstones, tile, and brick.
The only foot-prints in the snow, the dealer's, and his cat.
Him looking out for customers – the puss after a rat.
Both were disappointed, and huddled round the fire.
Darkness came, the clock struck five. Time then, to retire.
Lock the Architectural Salvage Yard, and write December off.
Beans on toast, not turkey. From the darkness came a cough...
"Excuse me," said a hearty voice, from somewhere in the blizzard,
"I've heard that when it comes to matching bricks, you're the local wizard." The dealer hadn't sold a brick all month, but clicked the padlock tight, (These customers at closing-time were never worth a light.)
"I'm sorry, mate," the dealer groaned, "I'm shut now 'til new year." But while the wind and snowstorm moaned, the stranger ventured near. "I need four matching chimney pots, three hundred handmade brick, and about a thousand Dreadnought tiles, and I need 'em bloody quick."
The dealer's mental 'rithmetic summed up a thousand smackers,
(But half-past five? On Christmas Eve? Had this bloke got

the ackers?) "I'd like to help," the dealer said, "but the fork-lift battery's flat."
"Don't worry," quipped the stranger, "I'll take care of that…"
…the dealer gasped when he saw the stranger's ermine-trimmed red coat, and the cash pulled from his fur-trimmed hat. He counted every note.
A thousand quid in fiftys. Christmas come at last!
But the yard all pitched in darkness, and that ice-cold Arctic blast!
He went in search of jump-leads, and steeled himself for work –
But the sight he saw, defied his eyes – the whole yard gone berserk!
He swore he saw a gargoyle, which he'd had in stock for years,
Walk past him with two chimney-pots, the snow still on its ears.
A pair of leaden cherubs somehow freed from off their stands, were flying past on leaden wings with tiles in their hands, while a crumbling compo Venus, her arms long amputated, hobbled by with a chimney-pot crown to where the stranger waited.
A swarm of brick were hopping through the yard right at his feet, carried by the brick's own frogs, a-leaping t'ward the street. … back and forth the cherubs, now assisted by stone doves,
and a barrow full of Dreadnoughts pushed by worn-out safety gloves.

And then a voice beyond the gate: A "Thank you!" boomed

out jolly.
The dealer stood, amazed and dazed, but keen to count the lolly.
The only sound above the wind, a clattering of hooves...
The only sight some tail-lights, that faded o'er the roofs.
...and all around, the yard stock-still. The snow-fall undisturbed, on bricks, on tiles, on chimneypots! The dealer all perturbed, unlocked the office, pleased to see the stove still worth a poke, so counted cash, and poured himself a hefty Scotch 'n' Coke...
...and woke to find his socks on fire! A newspaper had slipped
from off his lap, the careless chap. God knows how long he'd kipped, but the headline on the paper made this caper seem more daft — "Local house has chimney clipped by mystery air-craft."
At once his mystery customer was, apparently, in dreams.
The empty wallet evidence of all not as it seems,
Missing stock. And tyre-tracks. A Ford, a Merc, a Volvo?
Stolen: Statues, gargoyles, bricks... a Christmas list for Salvo.

Venus Rising from the Dung-Heap

She really was the finest that was ever laid in bed.
Not only a good looker, but apparently well-bred.
And worshipped from the moment that he got to sow his seed,
she responded to his tenderness, well-satisfied indeed.
Her skin would glow with pleasure as he massaged in the lotions,
while he plied her loving measures of mysterious love potions,
'til she'd blossomed all voluptuously to a plump, curvaceous form,
that her idoliser, none the wiser, thought to be the norm.
Lying resplendent in her bed, like a well-brushed Titian Goddess, the thoughts within her groomer's head were not of art, or modest! Pumped up the potions more and more, and bumped up the amounts,
but forgot the most unwritten law – it isn't size that counts.

For when, full-spent, his love-intent was alighted from her bed, in a two-man hammock just as if t'were Cleopatra instead; he saw the glory. End of story. Heaviest pumpkin. First! She'd been abused, was being used. She had no choice. She burst!

We Used to Play in the Hardest League of All...

In nineteen-hundred and eighty-seven, the blessed R F U
Issued forth a bold decree from Twickenham, HQ.
The professional era welcomed with a country-wide Blitzkrieg –
that henceforth on, all rugby clubs should take part in a... League.
No more the old "boot money" but some serious weekly dosh
with your Moseleys and your Coventrys all skint, all under the cosh...
And LEAGUES to be the measure of a rugby club's performance.
There's never been a fuck-up in a sport, of such enormance.
Decades on, our game evolves, but the witless RFU
has upped a side from just fifteen, to one of twenty-two!
From full-back through to hooker, plus a bench of seven subs,
so the third team now sits on the bench, in village rugby clubs!
A league success becomes the must; it's neither bust nor shit.
Wasp's sponsors cough up millions, Claverdon's buy the kit.
But Wasps can play their lifelong rivals, each and every season,
while Claverdon play strangers. There ain't no rhyme or

reason.
Who cares what league that Shipston play? We couldn't give a shit.
Three leagues up, we'd give 'em some, and that's the brunt of it.
Southam, Chipping Norton, Stratford, Standard, wankers all,
The RFU has ruled we can't contest them for the ball.
Little Johnny dripping-snot, from Claverdon's under-nines
will never know the rivalry the modern game declines.
He'll never get to know the bloke he's just kicked black and blue,
or the club, old fuck-knows who-eians; (That the Sat-Nav took him to.)
God bless those gormless old-farts in their blazers at HQ.
Pissed six sheets, in corporate suites. We wear blazers, too!
We run on bar-take, sponsors, volunteers with nought to gain.
Our crowd don't have a grandstand – just cow-shit, mud, and rain.
…and every game's a friendly, or at least come final whistle.
League or not, our blood and snot's from graft and honest gristle.
If your leagues can give us Oppo we can play year in year out,
our points awarded in the bar, you might just have a shout.
If the Leagues can make one fixture to look forward to all year,
and make it happen once a week, they might be getting near.
And little Johnny dripping-snot might get to love the game –
Three points a win, and bonus points? It's not the fucking same.

T M Smith

It all comes down to That Man Smith – The Ashes, in '19.
Take Smith's innings from the score, there was no Baggy Green with any Ozzie swagger that might be called a threat. The finest bowler in the world! Did his job on us, and yet…
It all comes down to That Man Smith.
He came here with convictions – though we knew he'd served his time, the crowd turned up with sand-paper, and mocked with chant and rhyme. It all came down to That Man Smith. The wickets fell around,
our bowlers bowling all their worth. But he knocked them out the ground.
It all comes down to That Man Smith.
We lost The Fortress. Drew at Lords. Then Stokesy won the third. (The only Test with "That Man" out. Concussed, the Docs concurred). It all comes down to That Man Smith. You've got to take him out, by guile or just plain G B H, to be within a shout.
Freak or genius, now compared by Ozzies with "The Don!" Greatness born? Not yet achieved, but no doubt thrust upon.
It all comes down to That Man Smith. The Fourth test, Ozzie heaven – Gets a couple on the helmet; gets 211.
It all comes down to That Man Smith.
No man, they say's an island, but he's an island in his team. A castaway. The Coach's curse, but every Captain's dream –

A man who breathes and sleeps and dreams of nothing but his cricket.
Can hit the stands but keep in hand his all-too-precious wicket.
It all comes down to That Man Smith.
A coach's bloody nightmare: and a pleasure all the same.
He's not come from the text-books, just lives the bloody game.
He knows he's got his team-mates – but out there in the crease, he's seeing things that we don't see – like a cat that's thick with fleas.
It all comes down to That Man Smith.
In Test Cricket there's no finer drill for measuring the spine and character of batsmen, than a spell of length and line,
but "that man" Smith despatches or dispenses each ball clean – 'twixt a mix of tics and twitches, tricks, and boundaries in between. It all comes down to That Man Smith.
Come The Oval, Smith gets eighty – and the Ozzies are on the rack.
There's big difference in a Series Win, or the urn just coming back.
The target set: but take no bet on a Steve Smith double-ton!
So to catch him out on twenty three meant at least this game was won.
It all comes down to That Man Smith.
For an Ozzie there's no limbo worse than ending up a draw.

It sticks with 'em like a Gipsy's curse, or an ever-open sore.
Serve 'em right. Bowlers, batters, grafted: we gave as good as got.
But it all came down to That Man Smith. And Bradman he was not.

Black Country Bacon

Yo c'n blart like a babby at what we'm all lost
from the Black Country's long list o' skills.
Yo c'n blart all yo like, but what's bosted is bost – They'm all
gawn from these rollin' dark mills.
The chainmekkers, brickmekkers, nailmekkers, all.
The foundry the forge, an' the mill.
The steelyards, the kilns am all gone t' the wall, an' the
wharves on the cut am all still.
Bosted or broke, a Black Country bloke
still needs summat good for 'is tay,
'an them as 'oo nourished them Black Country folk am alive
an' all well to this day.
The Pig-men ay lost, their trade am'nt dyin'!
They'll tell yer that business is great.
The pig-man – not 'im 'as once lugged about iron but 'im as
'oo cuts up the mate.
Sossidges, faggots, haslet and brawn,
the chops an' the 'ocks an' the belly,
Black puddin' n scratchins, an when it's all gawn, there's
drippin' that's drippin' wi' jelly.
But that ay all either, so copolt o' this –
'cos I do' want my praises mistaken;
Any imposters am tekkin the piss –
They know 'ow to smoke 'n cure bacon.
The smoke from the faggots, sawdust and sticks

Is a secret itself, to these men
'an ow long they ang 'em up – sometimes for wiks is a salt
'n' erb secret, again.
So do' blart like a babby next toime yo mourn
The passin' of black country craft.
Jus' try some smoked bacon – and if yo'm still sworn, then
I'm sure that yo must've gone saft.
There ay no denyin' there's lots bin forsaken
An' lost as the centuries go by
But mate, I can tell yo' that Black Country bacon is the
foinest that money can buy.

Done the Crossword…

I've done the crossword, just to keep the brain-cells on the go, but one clue I got stuck on, was a teasing so-and-so.
Left me puzzled. Just four letters. (Something) U N T *"Every maiden has one (4)"* The answer clear to me. "AUNT!" The Mrs answered, but I'd filled the bugger in. "Er, have you got a rubber?" I enquired, with a grin.

Bee's Knees on Holy Ghost

There's no finer feast that has fewer ingredients
for maximum taste out of quickest expedience.
You could bugger about with a packet or tin
with no guarantee of enjoyment within,
just an e-numbered quick-fix with zero content
but there's one instant supper, tea, lunch... heaven-sent.
The tools that you need for the snack of your life are *a)* just
a grill, and *b)* just a knife.
The ingredients are simply remembered, with ease – a) any
bread, and *b)* any cheese.
The bread white or brown, stale, mouldy, or fresh, and
cheese off the mousetrap will do — at a stretch.
Just whack up the grill-knob as far as it goes
Bung in your bread, then just follow your nose;
There's a smell when bread's toasting that says it's spot on:
Then, cheese! Whether grated or sliced, bung the lot on.
Grill bubbling golden, then tip onto plate –
The anytime banquet – cheese on toast, mate.
Condiments dictated by larder, or mood –
A bespoke-tailored dish, but convenience food...
Heinz ketchup, or Daddies, or mmwah! Worcester sauce.
Chutney or relish. Branston pickle, of course.
Best knife and fork, or just stuff in your gob.
Cheese on toast, anytime, mate – just the job.

Sweet Thoughts

I'm hankering for Bluebird Chocolate toffees… or a slab of peanut brittle.
Thornton's Chocolate Toffee rolls
Stuff I ate when I was little
A great big bar of nougat
American hard gums
Everlasting Strips
Sherbert dips
Stuff I got for doin' me sums
I want Nuttall's Mintoes
Toffee Eclairs
Rhubarb and custard
Jargonelle Pears
Dubble Bubble Chewing gums
Toffee apples
Candy floss
Gooey Puff Candy
Seaside Rock
Gobstoppers
Swizzells lollipops
Black Jacks (four a penny)
I'd love three penn'orth of Mojo's
Fruit salad
or a Lucky bag
but what I crave for, I suppose, is teeth! I've hardly any.

It's a Wrap

Spuds used to come in great big sacks
Now they come in vacuum-packs
Our ham and bacon from the slicer (which is why it tasted nicer)
Now it's rubbery, elastic,
And sweating, hermetic'ly sealed in plastic.
Biscuits, sugar, rice, were loose, their paper-bags put to good use.
Now, all their wrappings in the bin…
With a bin-bag, too, to wrap them in.
The compost-heap took all the scraps;
Now we buy compostable wraps… to throw the peelings in the bin!
Waste wrappers for waste packagin'.
Every dog-turd now gets bagged –
No wonder this ol' planet's shagged.
And what a stupid price to pay;
To buy this shite to throw away!

Love Hurts

Mary and Gladys was widders, both their 'usbands lost in the war.
'n' best o' mates, when yer considers they'd been gone forty years, or more.
They busied 'emselves at the Chapel, where they dusted and done all the flowers, spent afternoons playin' Scrabble 'n' Cribbage, 'n' Dommies, jus' passin' the hours.
On Sundays, post-Chapel, they'd go Midland Red 'n' tek in available sights;
they'd natter, 'n' gossip, 'n' rattle along, 'n' put the ol' world unto rights. Barr Beacon; The Lickeys; 'n' Malvern. 'n' sometimes a Chara to Rhyl! The Birmin'ham Museum and Art Gallery, or Cannon 'ill Park fer a thrill,
But come first Sunday in Michaelmas, they 'adn't got nothin' much planned.
When Gladys suggested, "Ow about Dudley Zoo?" Our Mary simply said, "Grand!"
They'd a penny arcade, 'n' the bingo, 'n' the tea-rooms did a cream tay,
'n' rhinos, 'n' crocerdiles, 'n' helifants. Hanimals frum far ower the say!
They strolled and cajoled, just 'avin' a laff, 'n' a man wi' a camera popped out, 'n' said, "Two and six for a photograph?" But with our Gladys's hearing in doubt, Mary said, "Stand still now, our Gladys. He's goin' ter focus. D'yer

see?" "Bloody hell!" says our Gladys. "What? Foke us? D'yer mean the both on we?"
The photograph taken, and five bob forsaken, and chucklin' all o' the way,
They'd jus' the chinchillas, the mountain gorillas 'n' off to the tay-room fer tay!
The Rwandan gorillas were really, quite thrillers. Gladys said, "Jus' look at 'is neck!"
Mary simply agreed. Waved 'er 'ankie, Coo-eed. "E's jus' like my Ernie. By 'eck!"
But, excusing your pardon, the gorilla got a hard on. "Jus' look at it, Glad, if you will!" Gladys was mesmerised by the girth and the size. "I tell you, it could be my Bill!" But as they gawped from over the parapet, poor Mary let go of 'er 'at...
It dropped right by the gorilla. Mary hitched up her skirt. "I'm buggered if e's 'avin' that!"
She jumped over the top of a near ten-foot drop and landed square on her feet. For a septuanagarian Presbyterian, I tell thee, one hell of a feat!
"It's only an 'at!" screamed Gladys, "Look at..." The gorilla had eyed up our Mary.
With lust in his eyes, and ten times her size, our old girl's situation quite scary.
He didn't mean no alarm, but his simian charm meant fuck-all to a Black Country wench.
And he ravaged her, savaged her, downright well shagged her, doggy-style over a bench.
While up on the pavement, Glad stared in amazement as the gorilla delivered its length.
Just like her ol' Billy, his wonderful willy a-glist'nin; Said

Glad, "Gimme strength!"

The zoo-keepers came, and to their rotten shame, they beat off the beast with their sticks.

An ambulance next. And my, was Glad vexed! For the tea-rooms were all shut by six.

Mary off to 'ospitle. Sittoo-ation critical. 'Er new 'at was all torn up 'n' tattered –

She'd gone through it and chewed it, bit 'tween 'er teeth, while the gorilla her vittles had battered.

Thirteen weeks in a coma (but a smile on her face) there were times when her life was in doubt; as from childhood and through widowhood, her dear old Glad stood by her bedside throughout.

"Oooooh! You poor soul Mary dear, whatever did 'e do t'yer?" Said Gladys, "does it hurt!" ...and Mary, elbows on her bed, putting in her dentures said, "Jesus, Gladys, does it HURT?"

"I'll tell you how it hurts, dear Glad. He spoiled my 'at! I'm 'oppin' mad, 'n it's onny just the start. He doesn't write... He doesn't phone... Not a single call... Ooh, Glad! He's broke my heart!"

Never Judge a Book by Its Cover

The receptionist at the agency was thinking life's a bore,
when she heard a sort of scratching coming from the office door,
so, when she'd filed her nails, and still the scratching going on,
she sashayed to the office door, and clapped her eyes upon...
A dog. A wiry thing, tongue hanging out and panting fit to bust –
and when it wasn't panting, it licked its arse of crust.
"Can I 'elp you?" said the receptionist, "I'm nearly off my shift."
"Yes you can," says the dog, "I'm knackered. Could you fix the fucking lift...?
I need a job. Your agency was recommended by my Vet.
Yes, I can talk. Queen's English! I can communicate, no sweat!"
The receptionist turned upon her heels, and burst in on her boss –
screamed, "Boss we've got a talking dog...!"
He couldn't give a toss.
"I've heard 'em all. Talking dogs, and parrots, gimme a shilling
for any animal that could talk, and include my wife god willing,

so take 'is number, sod 'im off, and find me something new…"

The dog skipped in, jumped on the seat, asked, "Any chance a brew?"

The agent fell back in his seat, and declared, "This dog's got class!"

"What's your name?" he asks it, "… and stop licking your arse."

"Fido," says the dog, then adds "and before you might enquire;

I 'aven't got no GCE's, no certificates or ref'rences, Squire."

"A talking dog! The Holy Grail! You'll never be out of work! You'll start at the Palladium! The crowds will go berserk! Seven nights a week, and matinees, and doing nowt but chat. I'll pay you more than Bruce Forsyth. What d'you think of that?"

The dog had took to scratching at some fleas around his knob,

but stopped to answer briefly, "I came here for a job! You're offer sounds amazing, but I tell you, it's a bummer… The whole lot means fuck-all to me. I'm a fucking Plumber!"

Do They Know It's Autumn?

It ain't gone October, and on the TV
Is the first Christmas advert. Jesus! Fuck me.
With the shelves still piled up with Halloween shit –
The pumpkins, the outfits, the trick-or-treat bit
and fireworks yet! There're months of activity
Before we get to the first kids nativity.
Your sofa delivered by Christmas, all right!
No need for them telling us ten times a night.
Kevin the Carrot's campaign's made a start
with Robbie Williams singing his part,
his soul and his song sold to fill Aldi's coffers.
"Let Me Entertain You" with our special offers…
Last year t'was our pleasure for Sir Elton John; to see the song that he sang was ours: gone! "Your song." Yes, mine! Elton told us! So who is my song's new co-owner? Who is John Lewis?
Christmas! It's here, shoved right in your face.
Grottos and reindeers all over the place.
To think that we've got almost eight weeks of this; for a big turkey dinner? They're taking the piss.
Brain-wash us with anthems until we are numb, all of 'em fighting to kiss Santa's bum
and fill up our stockings with plastic landfill
at the time when our by-line should be only, goodwill.
M&S have hijacked Fleetwood Mac

Turned Albatross into a Christmas track.
Argos kid's drum-kits have backed Simple Minds to drum up fuck-knows-how-many £79.99's.

All My Worldly Goods with Thee I Share…

Me and my ol' Mrs
have worn false teeth for years.
At night they soak, in dishes
labelled "his" and "hers".
Then one day when out sea-fishin'
I come over all sea-sick,
'n' found me gnashers 'ad gone mishing – Gawn somewhere
wiv Moby Dick.
When you're always short o' coppers,
'n' you're drinkin' on the slate,
A bran' new set of choppers?
Out of the question, mate!
One night when she was sleepin'
I thought, 'ang on, wait a bit…
I tried the Mrs dentures in,
And bugger me, they fit!
"My worldly goods, with thee I share…" She's a good old
stick, all right.
I 'ave 'em when they're going spare,
She 'as 'em bingo night.
I wears 'em for the snooker club
She wears 'em for her hair do.
I wear 'em quiz night at the pub,
I tell you – it's a fair do.
She 'ad 'em for 'er Sunday Church

'cos she couldn't face the vicar,
Then I 'ad 'em back for Sunday roast
'as I 'as my beef sliced thicker.
One Monday night she upped and died,
while I 'ad 'em in for Darts.
I gnashed 'em, while I did decide
if death really does us parts.
With teared eyes, I gave her teeth
to the appointed undertaker.
I couldn't think, six foot beneath,
and about to meet her maker,
that she should not look beautiful
when rested in her peace –
So I handed 'em over, dutiful –
as they were 'ers, not mine, at least.
The funeral done, and everyone
said she didn't half look a treat.
She did 'n' all, but said and done,
I'd 'ave to give up eating meat.
I stood beside her graveside,
when all of 'em 'ad gone –
When the Vicar come and stood beside,
'n' said, "These are yours, my son!"
'E handed me a yoghurt-pot –
and in it was her teeth!
The Vicar put me on the spot.
"They're yours. It's her bequeath;
Yours, not just for Darts on Monday,
but with your Mrs now with God,
You'll wear 'em here in Church on Sunday,
and it serves you right, you Sod."

So I pray each Sunday, for the Vicar.
I grins wide, 'n' blows 'im kisses –
It'll not get me to heaven quicker,
But God bless my dear ol' Mrs.

Grow Old Disgracefully

Hope I die before I get old!
We know what Daltrey means —
He's seventy five. All tickets sold,
still wearing them tight jeans.
Rattlin' tambourine to Townshend's riff.
Pensioner rock-stars! Then there's Cliff.
Satisfaction he can't get!
Mick Jagger's screaming so.
He's seventy nine. So what's the bet
it's arthritis on the go,
and his ol' snake hips completely stiff —
Pensioner rock-stars! Then there's Cliff.
Ozzie's screaming's not so loud
and the pigeon keeps its head.
He's seventy one. Still plays the crowd,
won't see head-banging dead.
Vegan. Almost teetotal, Man. Just an occasional spliff…
Pensioner rock-stars! Then there's Cliff.
They're still throwing knickers at Tom.
(as he still cuts a very fine figure)
At seventy nine, still sings Sex Bomb
but the knickers they're throwing are bigger. A corset contains his expanding midriff. Pensioner rock-stars! Then there's Cliff…

For his eightieth birthday, Cliff's going on stage
A teenager stuck in deep freeze.
No patina worn by the coming of age
of a rock star now brought to his knees.
No ravages of rock, nor roll, not drugs, not a sniff...
Sterile. Sanitary. Same old, same old. He's never had the Syph.
Iggy and "Keef" show every year
of their craggy, wrinkled-up chops –
good ol'-fashioned drugs sex and beer
and a couple of heart by-pass ops.
Arthritic fingers can still nail the riff –
Pensioner rock-stars! Then there's Cliff.
They lived the life, the dead rock stars
The ones we'd pay to see;
To hear live, imagine. All the young dudes... like Freddie Mercury!
Elvis would be eighty four. Otis seventy eight. I can't help wonder, "Oh, what if...?"
And each time I heard the news, I thought: Why couldn't it be Cliff?

(author's note follows)
Apologies, Mr & Mrs Rodger Webb -
I mean your son no harm.
His album sales aren't on the ebb
Your lad retains his charm.
He's Eighty now, a grown-up lad. A hit would be terriff, for Harry Webb, still a celeb, but also known as Cliff.

No Pets

Grandad came home with an elephant,
From a gypsy down the pub,
who'd lost his shirt at three-card-brag
and been denied the sub.
'twas Grandad who had won the pot
(with a pair of two's, for shame)
'n' the gypsy short on cash and beer,
'ad to settle for the game.
A bag o' peanuts in the pot
was all the gypsy threw,
explainin' it was all e'd got,
but "it" needed feeding, too.
The elephant filled up our back yard
wi' a tarpaulin for the rain
but the muck went on the rhubarb
so me Grandma dey complain.
He often took it up the park,
'cos it liked to chase a stick;
but it chewed up all the football pitch,
which got on the Parkie's wick.
You'd always see the elephant
stood outside some corner-pub,
Or waiting by the bookies,
Or the Burtons snooker-club.
An elephant in Dudley

soon hardly caused a stir,
Especially with me Grandma –
Now she knew where Grandad were…
So when she saw the elephant
Outside the barmaid's digs
(Instead of the allotment),
She was hardly dancin' jigs.
"It ran off with the Circus,"
was what my grandad swore
but from that day, the elephant
was never seen no more.

Saturday Cinema Club

We are the boys and girls well known as
The minors of the A B C
And every Saturday all line up
To see the films we like, and shout aloud with glee!
We like to laugh and have our sing-song
Such a happy crowd are we,
We're all pals together,
The minors of the A B C!

Our kid and me would never miss the Saturday morning flicks.
We all got in for sixpence each, instead of one-and-six.
We got there early, just for fun; we always jumped the queue, sliding down the bannisters, being cheeky, as kids do.
The commissionaire or "Uncle Bill" – an ordinary bloke would try to stop us running wild or climbing on the coke. "Who threw that? Who did that? Who swore? I'll tell your Dad!" Until the doors were opened, we all drove him bloody mad.
Uncle Bill up on the stage, the usherettes in the aisles, would scream and beg for order in a shower of missiles – Lollysticks and ice-cream tubs, half-chewed toffee bars
"... little bugger! I'll box your ears! I'll smack your bleedin' arse!"
The lights would dim, the curtains sweep, but not before the song – We yelled it, shouted not with glee, but a Gang-show

all gone wrong. We wrestled, dead-leg'd, scrapped away, the aisles stayed a scrum – ... for always first, the trailers of the features yet to come...
This Wednesday! One week only! The Blob! Certificate X!
...this trailer certificated U... (we hardly shat our kecks)
This Sunday! One day only! The Knack! Certificate X!
...this trailer certificated U... but the cartoons! came on next.
The Looney Tune brought a scramble, as each ran to his place, and any scrapping after got a torch shone in your face.
Shut up! Keep quiet! Stoppit now! Stop standing on the seats!
We'd clamber down. We'd fart. We'd laugh, with gobs chockful of sweets.
Wile E Cyote and Road-Runner; Daffy Duck & Elmer Fudd, Tom & Jerry, Bugs Bunny, Popeye – not one of them a dud, so when it came up, "That's all Folks!" we'd boo as fit to kill.
No lion-tamer in a cage so brave as Uncle Bill.
After cartoons came the serial – where the *start* was the best bit... to see just how our hero got himself out of the shit.
Last week the car went off the cliff. Our hero strapped inside. This week, he jumps out just in time. As if! The bugger died!
Flash Gordon. Zorro. Marvel-Man. The Rocket-Man, got out – of fires, floods and death-chambers designed to wipe them out. The baddies always bit the dust, the goodies always won. Hopalong Cassidy, The Cisco Kid rode off, in setting sun.
The feature films were past their best – mostly black and white. Abbott & Costello, Dead End Kids, we all thought they were shite, but we all laughed at them, Three Stooges –

Larry, Joe & Moe. The more we liked the feature film, the less stuff we would throw.

"Bill" once copped me: blinded, by his torch-light in the dark. "Shut up!" Shut up we did. Our Kid, next week, just for a lark, brought in a torch our dad had bought, one million candle-power and gave it Uncle Bill face-on – his shadow stayed there for an hour.

No Mums or Dads or teachers, just the usherettes and Bill. The films the cartoons, serials; which was the biggest thrill? The Looney Tunes? or rolling-on-the-carpet anarchy? ...The boys and girls well known as The minors of the ABC.

Back in daylight, through the streets, our heads still at the flicks, we baggsy'd all our hero's roles and fought it out with sticks.

"Play up your own end! Mind your lip!" would never bother Zorro.

I've sixpence left. A bag of chips. And Sunday school tomorrow.

The Barclays Banker

"Architectural Salvage Dealer. er, reclaimed bricks and stuff.
...I'd like an overdraft." A yawn. He'd clearly heard enough.
Years ago, my Manager was simply hard of hearing –
but the lad I cop for nowadays, has a tattoo and an earring.
He doesn't tap his hearing-aid, as Mr Hawkins did,
to indicate a courteous "no" to umpteen-thousand quid.
He cannot offer compromise, assistance. Just ticks boxes, his face a pimpled lunar-scape of adolescent poxes.
"I've got this deal. I buy at ten, and sell for forty two.
There's 50,000. Take two weeks. That's fifteen grand, to you.
I've got the Nelson-Eddies, but I need you, just in case..."
He looked as if his favourite aunt had just sat on his face.
Now, Mr Hawkins had his nerves, but always came up trumps.
He knew that flogging cobblestones was bound to have some bumps.
He didn't scratch his arse and go for filling in a form.
The architectural salvage trade, he knew, was nowhere near the norm.
He drove a Rover, liked his golf, had trophies in his office, with over-spilling ashtrays and cup-marks from endless coffees.
But now it's a "Consulting Room" where the snot-nosed hear our pleas, just a ten-mil plate-glass distance from the next guy on his knees.

I remember Mr Hawkins' joy when the cobbles came up good.
"Well done," he said, "well done, my boy." (He knew they bloody would) ... and so we prospered. Me, and no doubt Hawkins-and-the-bank. Jump twenty years. It's down to me, and couldn't-give-a-wank.
"...so, sales," he says (scratching arse), "what's in the order book?
Expecting any payments in? Is factoring worth a look?"
"No," I say, "I've got the dough. But sometimes it goes sour." His reply completely de rigeur, for one paid by the hour...
"We'll issue you a credit card. If stuck, you pay with that."
I HAVE TO PAY UP FRONT, IN CASH, YOU STUPID LITTLE TWAT!
He didn't bat an eye-lid. Just shoved me up a form.
"The architectural salvage trade," I said, "... it's sometimes off the norm..."
...but spotted Dick was rambling on, like a parrot high on speed. "There's X per cent for drawing cash, the rate will make you bleed. I send the form off – guaranteed, you'll know within three weeks." Oh, Mr Hawkins, please come back, and sack these spotty geeks.
We always need the cash up front, we in the salvage trade.
It might not fit the profile, but an honest bob is made,
...and who else can we turn to, when our moneys with the bankers?
A post-grad. Ear-ringed, with tattoo. I tell you, they're all...

£1,000 prize for completing the last word to this poem. Simply call 07709 0222002. Calls charged at £1.25 per minute, texts incur an arrangement fee of £25. Or log in to fukubankcorp.com for free, giving us every detail of your life for us to send on to other leeches.

155

Schneider Webster Esq.

Schneider der schpeider lies waiting for flies,
a hackneyed *arachnid* with dust in his eyes…
He's resting his legs, but his eyes *never* close –
Just in case there's a bluebottle under his nose.
Spiders like Schneider can ill afford sleep
With a wife and a dozen-or so kids to keep,
For a house-spider's life isn't easy, you know –
To be feared by all, the bigger you grow.
Schneider the spider lives under the sink –
Which is not such a nasty place as you think.
If you're a spider. It's cold, just a treat
For storing dead bodies of flies fit to eat,
And the odd daddy-long-legs wrapped up for later – It makes for a good spider-y frigerator.
But each time poor Schneider goes out for a stroll, that's…
2, 4, 6, 8 legs out the plug-hole,
An eight legged, black-kneed *arachnid* at that!
The size of a saucer, or I'll eat my hat!
Then we all scream! Aaaaagh! Look out! a spider!
…which is hardly good reason for squashing poor Schneider.
For who'll eat the bluebottles? Who'll eat the flies?
Schneider the spider does. Spits out their eyes,
After sucking them dry of their guts and their blood.
Kills creepy-crawlies, like house-spiders should.

And if that sounds disgusting, then just think of this – A bluebottle sips on the soup from corpses.
Then shits maggots who turn into millions of flies that will eat their own vomit right under your eyes…
Whereas Schneider the spider lives under the sink. Which is not much to ask, after all, don't you think?

Bluebells

Never trample bluebells or you'll get lost in the wood! The fairies dust your footsteps 'til the trail is lost for good.
The bluebells are the fairy bells that ring when you are near, and they tinkle out a tinkle-bell that only fairies hear.
But every time a bluebell dies, it casts a fairy spell and lost forever in the woods the careless ne'er-do-well.
And never walk in bluebells in the shadow of an Oak!
For you'll waken up the Oken-elves, the woodland's wicked folk
who'll spoil the crop, and sour the milk, will not be reconciled 'til summoned up the Succubus to sow a demon-child.
The bluebells paint the woodland glades that shade will later hue; and gone, the fairy new-born in the woodland leaf anew,
'til sunlight, lost through summer leaf and winter's ashen sky shines spring. Bluebells meet the sun and bow – a fairy passing by.

A Wagging Tale

Doggy's doo-doos
Poochy-poos
Pooper-scooper doggy-loos
Done his business
Did his bit.
Did his what?
Had a shit.
As dogs do.
Squat.
You know what?
We've lost the plot.
Commonsense
an offence,
Ladies and gents.
Official word:
Put the turd
in a plastic bag.
How absurd.
Ickle-wickle Nanky-Poo,
Lassie,
Bobby,
Scooby-doo
think we're barmy, me and you.

Telly Clerihews

Dancing on Ice
Take my advice –
Turn over quickly
if hoping for Strictly

Midsomer Murders
As totally absurd as
Murder She Wrote…
Where's the remote?

Casualty
Doesn't do it for me;
they've got staff in excess.
It ain't NHS

Holby City
Just as shitty
But has the X-Factor
for a resting soap actor

Michael Portillo
A likeable fellow
His *"Bradshaw's Guide…"*
is an enjoyable ride.

Vera
Queerer
than any female D.I. yet.
Older and wiser; wey-aye, pet.

Peaky Blinders
Leave painful reminders
While acting unlawful
their Brummie is awful.

Good Morning Britain
You'll hardly be smitten;
Piers Morgan's opinion
and Suzanna his minion.

Countryfile
Hands-on stile
Farming fully illustrated.
Ears pierced, bulls castrated

Antiques Roadshow
Priceless? Or so-so?
Found in a skip? left by Grandmother?
"We'd never sell it…" Tell me another.

Paul O' Grady
No longer a lady
His future is sunny
but just not so funny.

Jeremy Clarkson
Is known for remarks. Un-
politically correct. And the odd stunt.
My mates all like him. I think he's a clown.

Endeavour
is very clever.
And as John Thaw is dead, of course
We then get *Lewis*. More re-*Morse*.

Blue Planet
Who'd pan it?
Deep-see fantastic
Swimming with plastic

Covid Corner: Come Together

Aint got no bogroll, aint got man-size Kleeenex. Aint got
Paracetomol, aint got stuff to clean kecks. We get dirty looks
Each time we sneeze –
Stockpilin' and panic is a selfish disease
Come together! Right now. Covid nineteen.
These crowded places need to lose their footfall
Aint no Gee-gee-racin' aint no Euro-football
They can play, but they've
no crowd to please
Two metres apart, or just you do as you please Come
together! Right now. Covid nineteen.
Coronavirus it got joo-joo eyeballs
It got all blue meanies it one Holy roller
It comes on and on…
then on your knees
He'd like to say he's feelin' good but hear that cat wheeze
Come together! Right now. Covid nineteen.
We all got cell-phone, we got instant picture,
We got face-book pen-friends, we got instant getcha, we got
sad faced,
imoji's
Got to be the real thing not what someone else sees,
Come together! Right now. Covid nineteen.
He gotcha neighbours he got all your old folks
He got all them gaspers, he got all those long-tokes

Going down in ones
and twos and threes,
but see 'em on the subway they're all thicker than fleas
Come together! Right now. Covid nineteen.

Covid Corner: Save Your Kisses for Me

I always thought that double-kissing was completely mad but can't deny I'd double-kiss my long-departed Dad,
though I know what he would make of it – no need to second-guess; he'd say, "Get away, you soppy nelly, don't be such a Jess!"
The continentals can't get by without one on the cheek, and then one on the other chop, a thousand times a week.
Us Brummies don't give out much, you're never getting kissed.
You might just get a hand-shake and a grumpy old, "Ow bist?"
Italian blokes will kiss their mates more often than the Mrs
They'll tongue the centre-forward, even when he misses!
Meet their mates down the Trattorria, 'n' before you've wet your whistle, you've had a dozen face-fuls of garlic breath and bristle.
And look to where it's got us, when in China there's a pace of customaly gleetings, and lespect for gleet-ee's space.
A simple bow. No ripstick, with two smackers either side, yet Coronavirus raged through 'em like a buckin' bronco ride.
No wonder that the virus spreads when contacts at the heart;
I'll just hope and pray the Brummie way gives us a healthy start,
And if I never double-kiss again, it's hardly sacrifice,

so apologies to you woossie fans of not-just-once-but-twice.
Now listen in, you Englishmen! We can help to beat the bug!
Stiff upper-lipped, no handshake – and at last we've lost "the hug". The hug that's all American-boy, all "don't we love each other?" (A Brummie don't do hugs at all, with the exception of his mother)
If you don't kiss the dustman, it could save a thousand lives.
Save your hugs and kisses for your children and your wives.
Keep your distance, wash your hands (of course, you always do)
And think of this: Your mother-in-law's got f**k-all kisses due.

Covid Corner: What a Crazy World We're All Locked in

Mother's in the parlour, playin' on-line bingo,
Dad's on-line on the fruit machines, 'n' watchin' every spin go!
No-one seems to notice us, now we're all locked-in!
What a crazy world we're livin' in!
Now, the old man never talks to me, but now its noon and night:
I've only got to cough and 'E's concerned his lad's all right
Swears its Covid 19, rubs Vick into me chest,
And a great big bowl of rabbit stew. Gimme a bleedin' rest!
He should be down the dog-track, Ma should be down the bingo
We should all be drinkin' down the boozer. Where did all the Gin go?
No-one seems to notice us, now we're all locked-in!
What a crazy world we're livin' in.
Brown Bread!
Instead...!
Mother has took to bakin' and her baps are lookin' fine! (Or so I 'eard my father said, and 'e said they felt divine)
but they all came out like bowlin' balls, and easy twice as hard, she threw 'em out the window an' they bounced around the yard
Three weeks they've closed the dog-track. Three weeks they

closed the bingo. Can't even buy us fish and chips – where else would the win go?
Three weeks of just our own four walls, now we're all locked in, what a crazy world we're livin' in.
Yay!
Father's doin' press-ups, to a video on the telly
Pity 'e can't see the screen for 'is barrel of a belly
Mother's runnin' round 'im, an' exercisin' too,
after the cat that's run off wiv' the rabbit from 'er stew…
'cause we can't go down the dog-track, we can't be playin' bingo.
We gotta keep six feet apart, or how far will this thing go?
The NHS is bustin' guts – isn't it a sin?
What a crazy world we're livin' in
Yeah, what a crazy world we're livin' in
What a Covid-crazy don't get lazy
Weeks three, four, Gawd knows how more
of this crazy world we're livin' in.
Oy! …an' keep yer distance…!   What a Crazy *etc.*

With acknowledgement to Joe Brown & his Bruvvers. Great song.

Covid Corner: Track Your Delivery

White Van Man wears rubber gloves but the same pair all day long, and thinks they give protection but he couldn't be more wrong.
If your doctor did the same each day, he wouldn't get too far
– From arsehole onto tonsils, and we'd all be saying "aah!"
The parcels he delivers, after thirty, forty drops to lots of random doorways, odd offices and shops,
all double-wrapped by unseen hands in plastic; nothing worse, are a deadly pass-the-parcel game; your prize, this fucking curse.
So while we all stay safe at home, our loved ones far and wide, White Van Man still plies his trade, with more and more beside. Like bees that flit from bloom to bloom, and pollenate the flower, our White Van Man drops off, collects, the virus by the hour.
For fucks sake can't we do without our daily "necessaries"? The printer ink, the bargain buy, our cosmetic accessories, the stuff we have to order, 'cos we can't get to the shops? For White Van Man to carry-out. Let's hope the penny drops.
Bog-roll by the pallet-load: You can buy it all on-line
and the chancers that supply demand will all be doing fine,
pay White Van Man eight quid an hour; no doubt the bastard needs it.
Market-force demand or Covid's right hand? Either way, he

feeds it.

Do you really need it? Ask yourself before you press the button on the check-out for your shirt or party-dress. For White Van Man is waiting, for your order on his load – Coronavirus rocks; your party-frocks are on the fucking road.

Covid Corner: Burglar Bill's Overview on Covid-19

They're releasing all the burglars who are nearing end of sentence —
regardless of their good behaviour, nil-points for non-repentance.
(Just in case they get the virus while they're locked up in their cells!)
When we're ALL on fucking lock-in. But we don't get the bells.
Poor Burglar Bill, with two more months for him to do his time
 is heading for a punishment that doesn't fit his crime…
His home-coming party at the pub is banjaxed, for a start,
but it won't be long before he longs to hear his cellmate fart…
His Mrs won't embrace him with the passion he had planned; it won't be bed; he'll get, instead, a paint-brush in his hand,
and a list of jobs now he's got the time, but should he need fresh air,
there's a lawn that's four-foot high and two year's dogshit hiding there.
His mates are all locked in as well, so forget the get-together;
There's fuck-all on the telly, and no sport in any weather.
Can't even go a-burgling! Shit! The bastards are all in!

Claim Coronavirus benefit! Self-employed, and now locked-in.
Burglar Bill surveys the meal prepared for his homecoming.
Dino-burgers, pasta shells, and jam & bread forthcoming
It's Friday, when he'd get himself a tray of fish and chips,
Or a Halal meal. Lamb curry, naan, a selection of fresh dips.
He's got a cough. Dodgy baccy. Phones for an appointment.
And his piles are playing up again. Need to get some ointment.
You what? Four weeks? No quack? No prison doctor on demand?
Poor Burglar Bill, locked in again. He's left the promised land.

The BallyMacKenny Stud

'twas an emergency urgent meeting
of the BallyMacKenny Zoo.
They'd a thirty year old gorilla that
needed a seeing-to,
Or, as the Professor of the
Primates said, Gussie was in
season. She should have been in
menopause: He'd got no rhyme or
reason.

She was doing things that ladies shouldn't,
when desperate for a male Showing off her
reddened bits, fondling her swollen tits, far
beyond the pale. Erotic displays might
Attenborough amaze, but they had to draw
the curtain. Gussie, their dear old Orang-
Utang, was randy. That's for certain.

She could be declared pure Irish,
having got here three months old,
But Borneo was her place of birth,
and her lineage now stone-cold,
They'd searched the Orang-Utang dating sites
in hope of a perfect match, While Gussie kept
displaying, constantly playing,

with her curly ginger snatch.

With hoardings barricading off the Orang-Utang enclosure,
so no innocent eye could e'er
espy dear Gussie's rude
exposure, And announcements
to the local press that "Gussie's
ill in bed," The BallyMackenny
Zoo's accounts were plunging
in the red.

How long will Gussie's urge go on?
The zoo treasurer berated. The
Professor of Primates then
explained: once union
consummated! And added that, in
nature's way, should Gussie not get
stuffed... She'd see no use, curl up
and die: the treasurer wasn't chuffed.

But news came in that a merchant
ship, due in Belfast docks that eve,
carried a gorilla on a straight-through-
trip; just too good to believe.
Destined for a circus in Florida,
they'd make sure he got shore-leave,
for a dirty weekend in BallyMackenny,
and Gussie's needs relieve.

But that night, upon the gangplank
of the M.S. Enniskilling,

the skipper gave them news that
though the gorilla likely willing,
as he'd always been chest-
thumping, and always in a rage…
but just about three weeks ago, was found dead in his cage.

"They shouldn't send wild animals
with no-one to escort 'em. We're
supposed to keep his body chilled,
pending a Post-Mortem but he
wouldn't fit in the freezer so we
buried him at sea."
The captain showed his paperwork. No mate for poor
Gussie.

The night was freezing cold, and
dark, so they found a Quayside Inn;
A clearly rough establishment, but
nice and warm within.
Three Guinesses were ordered,
with three Jamiesons on the side,
The BallyMacKenny committee's
quest had well and truly died.

They sat there with their heads
in hands, clearly in despair
When a ruckus started at the
bar, and foul curses split the
air – A boiler-stoker, on
shoreleave,
 had been refused a drink;

His shore-pay spent and his slate expent!
But... a gorilla, if you blink.

A shock of curly ginger hair, and close-together eyes.
A Simian chin and a flattened
nose, and one helluva feckin'
size! Barrel-chest, in a beer-
stained vest, his huge fists by his
knees, like great big dangling
lumps of ham; a gorilla, if you
please!

A quiet word with the barman, and
they cleared ol' Paddy's debt,
supplied him more ale, and told
their tale; he broke into a sweat.
"In case you're fussy, here's a picture of
Gussie." A glint came in his eye. "Gagging
for it, so she is," the Professor said, "We've a
feather bed put by."

"She's a lovely lass," her keeper uttered, "and I'll
scrub her up all clean."
"You've never had your bread so buttered, said
the treasurer. we're not mean... There's a 500
Euro Stud Fee... no doubt we can keep you in
beer..."
"Well," Says Paddy, "one heck of a shout. A minute. I've
come over queer..."

Yer man swallows his pint, looks at the
snap. Wipes his gob 'n' says… "I'll do it!
But I must set conditions on this, me ol' chap,
before I feckin' go through wi'it.
He scratches his head. "she's a beauty, well said,
but I can't be doin' wi' kissin'"
so we'll get on instead with my duty. In bed. The foreplay
will have to go missing."

…'n' there's the off-spring. If so,
then a Catholic up-bringin's for certain.
No televisions while I'm on the go, I
insist on having a curtain.
 …'n' just one more t'ing. I hope you don't think me
ungrateful or tryin' to be funny;
  The shaggin' bits fine. But it'll take me some time, to feckin'
come up with the money!"

Foul Play

If you like a Lincoln
sausage, or a good ol'
Barnsley chop, then I beg
you take advantage of
Taplow's butcher's shop.
On the corner of the
Market square, and Abattoir
street, you'll get no finer
local fare; Ol' Taplow
knows his meat.

He's Melton Mowbray pork-pies,
and Cornish pasties, too. Aberdeen
Angus burgers, and shin-beef for
your stew.
Gloucester old-spot
bacon, smoked out back,
in't shed and always in
the window, a fully
dressed pig's head.

One day as Ernie Taplow wire-brushed his block,
A rather stout old duffer entered:
sniffed the air, took stock... And
enquired, that he was looking for

a large Aylesbury duck. "Far end
of the counter! There's half-a-
dozen. You're in luck!"

Ernie eyed the fat old bugger,
who was eyeing up the birds…
His customer's inspection just
left him stuck for words.
Two fingers up the stuffing-
end, then wave them in the air
– And sniff the aroma left
behind, then curse, as in
despair.

He fingered all six ducks three times,
then triumphantly exclaimed, "These
ducks don't come from Aylesbury! They
shouldn't be so named." Our butcher
eyed the customer up, (with his good
name now in question), said, "I know
where all the ducks were raised. Here's a
suggestion…"

Ernie Taplow dropped his strides, and his long-johns to his
feet,
and bared his arse – his ring, at that –
to the customer (and the street). "Be
gentle, Sir, please do your best. I'm
desperate to see;
Where was I born? 'Cos if you know, you're a wiser man
than me."

The Cricket Match

Ol' Tom had done the boundary-rope,
and the creases all were marked; The
sight-screens were in position, and the
heavy roller parked.
The young un's practicin' in the
nets, an' us old 'uns in the Bar,
In readiness for a cricket-match,
we fortified with jar.

Our irreg'lar Wednesday evenin'
team, of all our odds and sods –
Them as jus' likes a game
o'cricket, regardless of the odds.
Ol' Tom was once on County's
books, a more than handy bat,
'til his tractor run 'im over. A
gammy leg, 'n that was that.

Our quickie is a Blacksmith, who's lost three of 'is
fingers,
You'd not want one in the
knackers from 'is legend'ry in-
swingers. We love these summer
tourists, you never know what
you'll get – A pub side, or a village

team, or some toffs from the
County set.

Cricket at its best, good as any Lords
Test. A match of willow v leather, of ball
v bat, what comes of that, then getting
pissed together.
"So who's our opposition?" asked the skipper; fair
enquiry –
We shrugged as one. "K218B," it said, in t' Fixture
Secretary's diary.

The church clock struck four, or attempted to, as it
stopped when just struck two, while the sky went as
black as nutty slack, and all the fuses blew.
We sat in darkness. Where was the
sun? Vanished from the sky. Thank
God we had some real ale pumps. At
least we'd not run dry.

We feared the end of the world,
we did; Surely, Armageddon. The
birds had all stopped singing,
every mobile phone a dead 'un.
The corrugated iron 'on't Pavilion
roof began a-rattlin' 'n' a shakin'
and we watched the cricket-square light up, jus' like
dawn was breakin'.

The tremors stopped – and then, a
hummmm… an' out there, in the light, was

a short-arsed chap with a Gunn & Moore
bat, all glowing Persil white, and with the
bat, he beckoned that we should join him
on the park.
"He looks just like Brian Lara!" (let's face it – there's
always one bright spark).

We ventured out, us one and all, and
our bright spark was dead right – It
WAS Brian Lara! But five-foot tall, and
yellow-jaundiced in the light;
though when he spoke, he was NOT the
bloke with a sweet West Indian tone, more
like he was gargling marbles, through a dodgy
microphone...

"I'm *GargleGargle* the captain, from our planet, K218B.
If you've never heard of us, well –
you named it thus – not me. You've
surrounded us with satellites, so
we've took to watchin' Sky - And
Cricket – lovely cricket – is what
helps our time go by..."

"Well bugger me!" piped up Ol'
Tom, then 'e took off 'is club cap,
'n' presented it to Lara, saying
"Welcome t't club, old chap.
Now can you switch the lecky on? Assumin' you're the
Boss?
We can start to warm the pies up. Then we'll get on

with the toss."

The lights flickered in the clubhouse, and
we heard the distant cheer. Darkness still
all round about, but to the boundary,
crystal-clear.
Our umpires for this Wednesday night, the Vicar, with
his glass eye,
and the village queer with a nose for free beer who
'appen was jus' passing by.

The Toss

T' Vicar fished out his ol' Half-
Crown, and tossed it in the air…
It hovered, six inch off the
ground! We stared as it hung
there; "Heads!" said Brian Lara,
and th' Half-Crown did just that
– touched down to show our
Queen face-up. Lara said, "We'll
bat!"

"Oh, no you won't!" objected
Tom, "You're on my cricket-
square. If you want to win, you'll
toss again. You'll win it playing
fair."
So the coin was tossed, and again we lost,
and again, they chose to bat. "Fair play!"

said Tom. "At any cost, I'll not be taken
for a twat."

THE TEAMS

Thrupston Wednesday Social XI:

Tom Tanner, 'is lad, postman Javhindad, an'
the public schoolboys, (three). The Smithy,
Ted (Wickey) 'is boy Tad, plus our captain
(elected), and me.
In at Twelfth man, was cross-eyed young Dan,
selected of his love for cricket. He just loved to
play; would run the wrong way, saw two (not just
one) middle wicket.

Planet K218B Touring Side XI:

Brian Lara, Bob Willis! Viv Richards, Jacques Kallis!
Sachin Tendhulka, and Gayle! Shane Warne and Dale
Steyn, you'd hardly complain at the cricketing talent
on sale. You couldn't bat deeper, and their wicket-
keeper was M S Dhoni, no less,
and with Courtney & Curtley, to put it quite pertly,
a team any planet would bless. Umpires:
Percy Dodds B.Theo. D.D.
The bloke from the Florists. Don't ask me.

Bales on. Our fielders loosenin'
up; the bowlers shining t' ball.
The batsmen entering the field,

aye-up, this is some curtain-call!
Jacques Kallis and Brian Lara,
walkin' in on Thrupston soil!
(never mind they're only five foot
tall and glowing like a boil)

"Gentlemen. Play."
Kallis, Lara, Richards. All out for a duck;
They didn't know how to bat! Boycott's
Mum would have more luck. Wi' a stick
o' rhubarb, at that.
Five overs in, they were five for three.
And four of them were extras. Tendulka
got scoring, thankfully – his batting much
more dextrous.

He and Dhoni combined to nurdle, grind,
and made the score respectable, 'til a
feather-edge was caught behind, the nick
clearly detectable.
Up went the Vicar's finger, but
this Sachin wasn't walkin' –
Instead, he chose to linger, 'n'
he 'n' Dhoni started squawkin',

an' a screechin' 'n' screamin' rent the air like nothin' on
this Earth.
We nearly called the team in, right there.
Like a Banshee givin' birth!
Ol' Tom, in his confoundry, yelled
"You're Out! So shut your gob!"

Sachin shrugged, dragged his bat to the boundary…
and turned into a blob.

We demolished their lower order,
despite some stubborn stands –
Just lambs unto the slaughter, in
our Blacksmith's partial hands.
Our visitors posted forty runs.
And we'd twenty overs to do it.
Our close encounter, just begun; if only any of us 'ad
knew it…

Ol' Tom 'n' one o' the schoolboys opened up the
Thrupston battin'
The fielders makin' some queer noise, like
Jack Russells when they're rattin'.
First ball from Curtley Ambrose, Ol' Tom
hits him for a six.
Over the boundary rope it goes, and Ol' Tom's in't best
of nicks.

Curtley's second, a meat pie toss. Ol'
Tom clouts it to the boundary… When
it hits Woolworths Window, in mid-air.
Much to our astoundery. The ball
drops, can't cross, this invisible barrier
in mid-air
Ol' Tom jus' runs, wi' 'is gammy leg, 'n' th' umpire signs
a pair.

Ol' Tom looks down the wicket,

to Captain Lara, in Tom's Cap,
'n' says, "I'll now show you some
cricket. Just look on, ol' chap."
'n' then proceeds, in dabs 'n' dobs, to tick the
runs – a flick, a nudge, a nurdle:
'til the scoreboard showed we needed just
one: at last, the final hurdle.

Bob Willis was the bowler up: he'd
be ashamed of his counterpart;
Got Bob's hair, 'n' Bob's run-up:
but in miniature, for a start,
with an arm so slow, it could only go to the boundary
for a six -
If it hadn't 've hit Woolworths Window, (but the single
did the trick).

"Have That!" yelled Ol' Tom, a-wavin' 'is
bat. I told thee not to cheat! Th'umpires
took the bales off, 'n that was that. They
didn't like defeat!
No handshake or "fair play", they simply limped away,
towards the boundary-dark where they'd just melt
away, though one was heard to say "sod that for a
lark."

Two pies each! Was the victory cry, as
Brian Lara turned down tea, Aboard their
spaceship, we waved goodbye, to the
team from K218B.
The church clock struck two – the two

strikes due! - no longer was it dark! Above
us all, a sky of blue; and we stood 'n' we
listened to the lark...

Ol' Tom had done the boundary-rope,
and the creases all were marked; The
sight-screens were in position, and the
heavy roller parked.
The young un's practicin' in the
nets, an' us old 'uns in the Bar,
In readiness for a cricket-match,
we fortified with jar.

"Who's the opposition?" asked the Skipper; but they
never got to see,
for cross-eyed Dan, our twelfth-man nipper,
(with eyes straight as you and me!) "All come,
quick!" he was a-bawling, "Ol' Tom's dancin'
on the square!" Sure, Tom's dancin' was
appalling, but his good leg, now a pair!

And clappin' his approval, was our Smithy:
with five fingers on each hand; whose
three-out-of-ten removal, was back as God
had planned!
If they only knew, this motley crew, how each got his
great surprise –
It was down to me, the vicar could see, or he'd now
have two glass eyes...

I don't know why they kidnapped

me, for they never saw me bat,
but I'm now the coach for
K218B, and it's not so bad at
that...
I've to teach 'em how to throw and catch,
and bowl, and how to field, Teach 'em
sweeps and cover-drives, in exchange for
old wounds healed.

They say they'll not harm hide nor hair,
while I get 'em up to scratch, and Planet
K218B will play fair and square, come
the inevitable re-match:
It might take years! But I'm assured my fears,
are based on our time's worth - but they
swear that when the clock strikes five, I'll be
back on Earth.

The Church clock struck five, or attempted to, but
stopped when just struck three... When the sky went as
black as nutty slack, 'n' Ol' Tom says "Bugger me!"